DATE DUE

MY 28 '90			
APR 0 4 2008			

D1443066

SINISTER TOUCHES

THE DIAL PRESS   NEW YORK

SINISTER TOUCHES

THE SECRET WAR AGAINST HITLER

by Robert Goldston

Published by
The Dial Press
1 Dag Hammarskjold Plaza
New York, New York 10017

Library of Congress Cataloging in Publication Data

Goldston, Robert C./Sinister touches.

Bibliography: p.
Includes index.
1. World War, 1939–1945—Secret service.
2. World War, 1939–1945—Germany. I. Title.
D810.S7G62   940.54'85   81–65853
ISBN 0–8037–7903–8   AACR2

for Bill Moffitt and Steve Hewitt—
two sinister sons-in-law.

ACKNOWLEDGMENTS

The author wishes to thank Random House, Inc., for permission to quote from "In Memory of W. B. Yeats," from *Collected Poems of W. H. Auden,* edited by Edward Mendelson, © 1954 by W. H. Auden; and to express his gratitude to the following authors and publishers for permission to adapt material to be found in the following books: *Cynthia* by H. Montgomery Hyde, © 1965 by H. M. Hyde; *Madeleine* by Jean Overton Fuller, © 1971 by J. O. Fuller, published by East-West Publications, Holland; *A Man Called Intrepid* © 1976 by William Stevenson by permission of Harcourt Brace Jovanovich, Inc.; *Dieppe: The Shame and the Glory* by Terence Robertson, by permission of the Canadian publishers McClelland and Stewart Limited, Toronto; *Bodyguard of Lies* by Anthony Cave Brown, © 1975 by Anthony Cave Brown, by permission of Harper & Row, Publishers, Inc.; *Ultra Goes to War* by Ronald Lewin, © 1978 by Ronald Lewin, by permission of the Author and his agent, James Brown Associates, Inc.; *The Assassination of Heydrich* by Jan G. Wiener, © by J. G. Wiener, by permission of James Brown Associates.

CONTENTS

PROLOGUE/AN ENIGMA

On a warm, misty August night in 1938—one of those summer evenings in Paris when the air is touched by the fragrance of chestnut trees and charged with a hint of romance, adventure, and approaching thunder—two men made their unhurried way through the bustling crowds, the pastry wagons, flower stalls, magazine vendors, baggage handlers, and travelers who thronged the cavernous Gare de l'Est. There was nothing apparently remarkable about the pair: One was tall, very thin, middle-aged; the other quite young, short, stockily built. The cut of their tweed suits and, perhaps, a kind of detached superiority in their manner proclaimed them English to the flower girl who sold each a white carnation boutonniere—probably university dons on their way to spend the bank holiday weekend in Germany.

Their train awaited them on Track 10, its dark blue coaches brilliantly decorated with golden flourishes; above spotless windows was the gilded lettering *Compagnie Internationale des Wagons Lits & des Grandes Expresses Europeans* and, beneath the windows, in golden capitals, ORIENT EXPRESS. The long concrete boarding platform was a scene of good-natured confusion as blue-uniformed porters tried to maneuver racks of luggage through throngs of boarding passengers and those who had come to wish them bon voyage. There was a great babble of languages; there were many bouquets of flowers, not a few silver hip-flasks, some tears, much laughter, and a growing sense of excitement as departure time approached. For in 1938, when those who could still traveled by rail, the Orient Express was the most magnificent train in the world: Its thrice-weekly departures from Paris were events of some importance.

Anyone observing the festive atmosphere at trainside would never have suspected that all Europe was poised on the precipice of war that August weekend. Didn't these happy, well-dressed people realize that across the border in Nazi Germany Adolf Hitler was once again roaring blood-thirsty threats—this time demanding a large slice of Czechoslovakia as the price of peace? At this very moment, in the huge stadium at Nuremburg, many thousands of black-shirted SS troops were rededicating themselves amid military rites to the conquest of *Lebensraum* (living space) in the east, their voices raised in the *Horst Wessel* song and disciplined shouts of *Heil Hitler!* Did that gay crowd in Paris not know that the Czechs had rejected Hitler's demands and mobilized their army, and since Czechoslovakia had firm military alliances with Britain, Russia, and France . . . Yes, they knew all these things. They simply preferred not to think about the unthinkable.

The two Englishmen strolled by a series of cars placarded STOCKHOLM, passed another series marked ISTANBUL and finally boarded one of a series labeled MOSCU. Once across the Rhine, the Orient Express would divide into three sections; theirs would proceed through Berlin to Warsaw, their destination, and beyond. They followed a white-uniformed steward down the red-carpeted corridor of their car to a private compartment, ordered a bottle of Poméry champagne, and relaxed in the softly upholstered seats, which would later be converted into beds. Above their heads two suitcases were neatly stacked in the baggage rack: They had been checked through from London the night before. The muffled tones of a gong warned visitors to leave the train.

Precisely at 8:00 P.M., amid a hiss of steam and the powerful chugging of twin locomotives, the Orient Express began its journey to the east. Its luxurious cars were filled with vacationers, business men, diplomats, military officers —a fair cross section of Europe's wealthy elite—not to mention a few gamblers, prostitutes, and pickpockets rich enough to follow their natural prey in first-class style. And of course, if legend is to be believed, this fabled train carried at least a few secret agents—glamorous women, elegantly dressed men, bound on missions of great danger and deep intrigue. On this particular August night legend *was* to be believed, at least partially, for the secret agents were aboard, though no one would have described them as either glamorous or elegant. Dressed in rather baggy tweed suits, they were comfortably sipping their Poméry and discussing the weekend cricket matches back in London.

They were an odd and eccentric pair, these two English-men. The older man, tall, spare, bespectacled, was Alfred Dilwyn Knox. His father was the bishop of Manchester, one of his brothers a high Roman Catholic prelate, another the editor of *Punch*. Alfred himself was a mathematician (he had gone to Eton as a King's Scholar, then to Cambridge, where he'd become a Fellow of King's College). During the First World War he had joined the cryptanalytical bureau set up by the British Admiralty. There, with dozens of other scholars, he'd succeeded in breaking almost all the German diplomatic and military codes of that era. One of them, a three-letter naval flag code, he had solved while taking a bath. After that war he had stayed in cryptanalysis—now under the control of the British Foreign Office's Government Code and Cipher School (GC&CS), known fondly to its employees as the "Golf, Cheese, and Chess Society." A shy, unpretentious man, Alfred Knox was regarded (by the very, very few people who knew of his work) as the foremost code expert in the entire world.

His companion, the younger, shorter, and more burly man, was Alan Mathison Turing, his assistant at the GC&CS. Turing was regarded as an authentic mathematical genius. He too had attended King's College, Cambridge, where he took first and second place in Mathematical Logic. Upon graduation Turing went to America, where he studied under Albert Einstein at the Institute for Advanced Studies in Princeton. Turning down the offer of a permanent position at the Institute, he'd returned to England and joined the GC&CS. It was there that Turing began brooding about the possibility of constructing a "Universal Machine." This would be a machine that, when given the necessary information, would *imitate* the behavior of any other machine—or, as Turing explained, "A sonnet written by a machine will be better appreciated by another machine."

While his friends puzzled skeptically over the Universal Machine, they were also bemused by Turing's personality. He listened each night to a radio program called "Toytown" about the adventures of Larry the Lamb, discussing every detail of the plot with his mother by long-distance telephone. He often wore a gas mask outdoors during the summer because, as he explained to suspicious village policemen, it filtered the pollen. He wrote to people in a code that no one could decipher, and as war clouds gathered over Europe, he converted all his family's wealth into silver ingots, buried them—and then forgot where they were.

Such were the two men who were bound that August night on a secret mission that would alter the course of history.

It had all started the day before in London, in the office of Colonel Stewart Menzies, deputy chief of MI-6, the British secret intelligence service. MI-6, in one form or another, had existed for more than three centuries—ever since the time of the Spanish Armada, when Queen Elizabeth I's principal adviser, Sir Francis Walsingham, had created a cunning network of spies to "gather all the secrets at the girdles of the princes of Europe." Since England's power was naval and maritime, MI-6, though nominally part of the Foreign Office, had generally been under the control of the Admiralty. Its present head, known traditionally as "C," was Admiral Sir Hugh Sinclair. But Sinclair was an ailing man (he would die in November 1939), and he tended to leave matters to Menzies.

Britain's intelligence services, in all their labyrinthine complexity, had always been the preserve of that English aristocracy, whose right and duty to rule half the world remained, in their own minds, unquestioned. Menzies was a perfect example of the type. He had been born in 1890 into an enormously wealthy family whose members had been courtiers for generations. His mother was lady-in-waiting to Queen Mary, his stepfather a royal equerry with the title of Silver Stick—the person traditionally charged with guarding the king from bodily injury. Menzies's youth was spent amid stately homes and palaces and, of course, he attended Eton, where he excelled at foreign languages and in sports. But he did not go on to university; instead he joined the ultraexclusive regiment of Life Guards. During the First World War, after the Life Guards had been all but wiped out at the battle of Ypres, Menzies joined MI-6. Thereafter, like all MI-6 officers, he cultivated anonymity and, where that was not possible, the reputation of being an idle, card-playing, fox-hunting, club-dwelling, aristocratic playboy. In this he was so successful that many government officials and military leaders doubted his capacity. They need not have worried. Menzies was possessed of a keen intelligence, excellent judgment, and, above all, ruthless determination.

The ruthless determination was essential. For nearly five years now, Menzies had been on the track of one of the most baffling problems ever to face British Intelligence—the cracking of the new diplomatic and military codes adopted by the Nazis after they seized power in Germany in 1932. The problem was baffling because, unlike the codes used by all nations until that time, these were not ciphers devised by teams of mathematicians that could eventually be solved by other mathematicians; the new German codes were produced by machine, a machine appropriately named Enigma.

Enigma had originally been the invention of a Dutchman named Hugo Koch who had patented his "secret writing machine" in 1919. It was intended for the use of corporations who wished to keep business secrets from nosy competitors. But the idea was not a commercial success. It was not until 1933 that Colonel Erich Fellgiebel, chief signals officer of the German high command, decided that Enigma would be the perfect communications device for the new tactics of *Blitzkrieg* (lightning war) then being adopted by the *Wehrmacht*. Enigma looked very much like an old-fashioned office-model typewriter. It had an ordinary keyboard in front, but on top, where the keys would strike on a real typewriter, was a flat surface with another alphabet displayed in little lights. When an operator struck a key on the board (say, the letter *M*), a different letter (say, the letter *K*) would be illuminated on top of the machine. What had happened was that by striking the letter *M*, the operator had completed an electric circuit that followed a crazy and unpredictable route through a series of four rotors, then hit a reflector and was carried back through the rotors' wiring by a different route until it illuminated the letter *K*. The wiring of the rotors was so complex as to defy analysis. Furthermore one, some, or all of the rotors could be turned at any time so that the electric routes were completely changed. And if this was not enough, there was a series of plugs in the front of the machine that could also be changed at will and would again change the wiring routes. The message thus encoded could be dispatched by any means—radio was the fastest—to the operator of a similar machine. Provided he had set his rotors and plugs in the same position as those of the "sending" Enigma (a process known as "keying" the machine), he could simply type out the code and the process would be reversed; by typing the letter *K* on the keyboard, he would illuminate the original letter *M* above.

Enigma was rugged, portable—the smallest army units could use it—and, as Fellgiebel judged, absolutely impenetrable. For even the most brilliant teams of mathematicians would require reams of messages and weeks of study to decipher *one* of the codes, by which time the information gained would be useless. And Enigma could produce an infinity of different codes at a moment's notice just by rekeying the rotors and plugs. So complex was the machine's capability that it didn't even much matter if one should be captured by an enemy: Unless he had access to the ever-changing keying procedures, it would be useless. Nonetheless, the German Intelligence services took every precaution against an Enigma falling into unfriendly hands.

The Poles, well aware that they were among the intended victims of Nazi ambitions to create a new German empire in Europe, had secured one of the old commercial models of Enigma and set a brilliant team of mathematicians to solving its riddles. But the possible combinations involved in the commercial model were 3×10^{18}, and on the more complicated military model (which the Poles did not possess) the possible permutations would be about 6,000,000,000,000,-000,000,000—*six thousand million million million*. In the precomputer age the solutions involved were obviously beyond the physical capacity of any group of mathematicians, even supposing they could devise a series of equations to do so. Unless, of course, they happened to possess the German keying instructions for any given dispatch. This, for a while, the French had, for they too had a copy of one of the more primitive Enigmas, and a German officer was willing to sell them the daily keying instructions for large sums of money. But this happy arrangement lasted for only a few months before the *Gestapo* caught up with the luckless officer.

To MI-6 and the "Golf, Cheese, and Chess Society," however difficult the mathematics involved in solving the Enigma ciphers, it seemed obvious that nothing worthwhile could even be attempted until one of the advanced military models, to which the Germans had now added a fifth rotor, could somehow be obtained. The simpler Polish and French versions, about which MI-6 was well informed, would not do. But military models of Enigma were closely and efficiently guarded in Germany.

Then, in June 1938, Colonel Menzies received a report from one of his operatives in Eastern Europe, Major Harold Gibson. It seemed that Gibson had been approached through the British Embassy in Warsaw by a Polish Jew who refused to disclose his real name and who we will call X. X claimed to have worked both as a technician and a theoretical engineer in the secret Berlin factory where Enigmas were manufactured. He had been expelled from Germany because he was a Jew and he now offered to build from memory an up-to-date military model of Enigma for the English. In return he asked for £10,000 ($50,000), British passports for himself and his family, and residency permits to live in France.

At first Menzies regarded this report with extreme skepticism. It seemed too good to be true. Intelligence services were constantly being approached by swindlers of all kinds, and £10,000 was no small amount of money. And even if this X was not a swindler—indeed, *especially* if he was not a swindler—then how had he ever managed to get out of Germany? Why had the *Gestapo* not simply killed him? Was this not perhaps a complicated Nazi plot to mislead British cryptanalysts? By planting a false Enigma on MI-6 the Germans might neutralize British code-breaking efforts for a long time. Menzies and his associates debated the matter for several weeks while MI-6 agents throughout Europe investigated X and his background. Finally a set of questions was devised by the GC&CS, which Gibson was to put to X and were hoped would reveal whether or not the man was a fake. Late in August Menzies had X's answers. The cryptanalysts of the GC&CS pronounced them "promising" and Menzies decided to send two experts to interview X personally. If they were satisfied that his knowledge was genuine, they were to instruct Gibson to escort the Pole to Paris, where, under the watchful eye of the local MI-6 resident, Commander Wilfred Dunderdale, X was to build his Enigma.

The two experts chosen by Menzies for this mission were Alfred Knox and Alan Turing, which explains their presence aboard the Orient Express that warm August night as the crack train roared toward the east. After a superb meal—the dining cars of the Orient Express were the equivalent of a four-star French restaurant—they wandered up to the club car, seated themselves at a vacant table, and ordered two brandies. The car was only half filled, but the atmosphere was pleasant. An attractive young girl was playing "Dardanella" on a small black piano near the bar; conversation was subdued but punctuated with laughter. Knox and Turing had just finished their brandies when the train slowed and came to a gentle halt. Through the windows next to their table they could see, by the glow of a harsh light, a small station platform upon which waited several uniformed men.

"German border," Knox observed.

A few minutes later one of the French conductors entered the club car, followed by two black-uniformed, jackbooted Nazi officials and a small, thin man in a rather shabby raincoat. *"Messieurs, dames, vos passeportes, s'il vous plaît,"* the conductor announced. The piano and all conversation fell silent as the German border police passed through the car, examining each passport, questioning one or two people in a desultory way, then proceeding until they had reached Knox and Turing. The two Englishmen handed up their passports.

One of the uniformed officials flipped through the pages. "Herr Smith and Herr Brown," he muttered in guttural English.

"*Ces messieurs sont procédés à Varsovie* [Warsaw]," the conductor explained.

"Smith and Brown?" the man in the raincoat asked with a thin smile. He took the passports from the uniformed border policeman and thumbed through them idly. "Mr. Smith and Mr. Brown," he repeated softly, "such uncommonly common English names. I see that you are both teachers. It is extremely expensive to travel on the Orient Express—for teachers."

"A remarkably acute observation," Knox drawled.

The man's smile vanished. "And perhaps, Mr. Smith and Mr. Brown, you would care to explain the purpose of your trip to Warsaw?"

"As a matter of fact," Knox said languidly, "we would not. As the conductor has already told you, we're merely passing through your glorious thousand-year *Reich* and we wouldn't dream of actually setting foot in it. What we do outside your ever-expanding borders really isn't any of your business, is it? Now, if you'll just be good enough to give us our transit visas, we won't take up any more of your valuable time."

The man's lips tightened. Then, after a moment's hesitation, he muttered something to the border policeman and handed back the passports. The officer stamped each, clicked his heels, bowed, and returned them to Knox and Turing. The French conductor, an expression of relief on his face, led the Germans to the next car.

Turing's hands trembled slightly as he lit a cigarette. "They'll investigate now," he muttered reproachfully. "We've all of Germany to cross."

"Yes, of course they'll investigate," Knox said calmly. "And what will they find? They will uncover the dreary truth —that we're on our way to Warsaw to attend a five-day seminar in Mathematical Logic at the university."

"You might simply have told him all that."

"Yes. But how much better for them to discover it for themselves. Much more convincing."

"Well, you needn't have been quite so insulting."

Knox smiled. "Mr. Brown, when you've had the experience dealing with German officials that I've had, you'll realize that Clemenceau was right: They're always either at your throat or at your feet. Personally I prefer them at my lower extremities. Another brandy?"

Shortly afterward Knox and Turing returned to their compartment. The car steward had prepared their beds and after a last cigarette they turned in for the night, lulled to sleep by the softly swaying motion of the great train, the muffled click of its wheels along the track joints.

A few hours later the motion abruptly stopped and both men awoke. They peered sleepily through their compartment window into the darkness beyond. No station was visible: The train was halted alongside a highway amid open fields. A long black limousine was parked on the road, and in the glare of its headlights they could see several German policemen hustling a passenger dressed in bathrobe and slippers down the gravel embankment toward the waiting automobile.

"Poor bugger," Knox muttered.

The train had already started again and the scene swept slowly from view.

"There, but for the grace of God . . ." Turing intoned.

"You might give some credit to MI-6," Knox observed with a yawn as he went back to sleep.

The following morning, exactly on schedule at 10:30 A.M., Mr. Smith and Mr. Brown found themselves in Warsaw. They took a taxi to the Hotel Bristol, where reserved rooms awaited them—they had been instructed to avoid contact with the British embassy for reasons we will later examine—and then, like any proper tourists, they went to visit the Madame Curie Museum. While they were admiring a bust of the famous Polish scientist they were approached by a thin, stooped man with unruly black hair—X, who'd identified them by their tweed suits and somewhat faded white carnations. After asking X a few prearranged questions to establish his identity, Knox and Turing began to question him about Enigma. The three men talked softly as they made their way through the various museum exhibits, and their conversation continued in the sunshine of a stroll down the banks of the Vistula toward X's lodgings in Warsaw's Jewish ghetto. There they made their farewells to X, returned to the Bristol, and waited. Promptly at 3:00 P.M. the telephone in Turing's room rang. Knox answered.

"Yes, speaking," he said. "Yes, we've examined the merchandise thoroughly. We would strongly urge that you purchase ten thousand crates for immediate shipment to our Paris outlet. Yes, very pleasant indeed—we'll be staying on for another three or four days. Quite so. Good-bye."

Turing glanced at his wristwatch. "We've just time," he said.

The two men strolled down to the hotel lobby. As they handed their keys to the desk clerk, they informed him that they would be dining in their rooms later that evening, and would he be good enough to get them a taxi? They were going to visit friends at the university.

Outside the hotel, within the doorman's hearing, they ordered their cab to take them to the university district. But a few blocks later they apparently changed their minds, for the cab turned suddenly into a side street and roared off at high speed toward the Warsaw airport. There they leaped out, pushed through the crowds inside the terminal, showed their tickets, were waved through passport control, and boarded a flight to Danzig with only moments to spare.

The plane was an old Ford trimotor, rickety, crowded, and uncomfortable. It was no better than the planes that would carry them from Danzig to Copenhagen, from Copenhagen to Amsterdam, from Amsterdam to London. But as they fastened their seat belts, Knox and Turing reflected that if this mode of transportation was barbarous compared to the luxury of the Orient Express, it had one distinct advantage: It did not cross German territory. . . .

The Peace Diary

November 11, 1918/Armistice ends World War I.

June 28, 1919/Peace Treaties are signed at Versailles: Germany is disarmed. A League of Nations is established.

December 1921/The Civil War in Russia ends with the Communists triumphant. The United States refuses to join the League of Nations.

April 1922/Disguised German rearmament begins.

October 30, 1922/Benito Mussolini, head of the Fascist party, becomes absolute dictator of Italy.

January 21, 1924/Lenin dies. Josef Stalin succeeds to power in the Soviet Union.

October 29, 1929/Prices on the New York Stock Exchange collapse. A worldwide Great Depression begins.

September 18, 1931/Japan invades Chinese Manchuria.

January 30, 1932/Adolf Hitler, head of the Nazi party, becomes dictator of Germany.

March 14, 1932/Franklin D. Roosevelt becomes President of the United States.

July 1934/Stalin seeks alliances with Britain, France, and the United States against the Nazi menace. The western democracies reject the Russian overtures.

June 1935/Fascist Italy invades Ethiopia (Abyssinia). Britain and France protest.

July 18, 1936/The Spanish Civil War commences.

October 1936/German armed forces reoccupy the German Rhineland and begin constructing heavy fortifications along the French border. France and Britain protest.

November 15, 1936/Italy and Germany sign "Anti-Comintern Pact" against Russia. The "Axis" alliance is born.

July 7, 1937/Japan commences an undeclared war against China. The United States and Britain protest.

March 12, 1938/Nazi Germany annexes Austria. Britain and France protest but take no action.

September 29, 1938/Meeting at Munich, Germany. British and French leaders agree to Hitler's seizure of the Sudetenland region from Czechoslovakia. Hitler proclaims this to be his "last territorial demand in Europe."

March 16, 1939/Hitler seizes all the rest of Czechoslovakia.

March 21, 1939/The Fascist armies of Generalissimo Francisco Franco enter Madrid.

March 31, 1939/Britain and France "guarantee" the territorial integrity of Poland against German attack.

August 23, 1939/Nazi Germany and Soviet Russia sign a "Non-aggression Pact."

DRAGON SEEDS

1

In the nightmare of the dark
All the dogs of Europe bark
And the living nations wait
Each sequestered in its hate.

W. H. AUDEN,
"IN MEMORY OF W. B. YEATS"

On that sunny August weekend in 1938 when Knox and Turing made their round trip to Warsaw, Mr. Winston Churchill, a Conservative Member of Parliament, addressed a gathering of his constituents at an open-air meeting in Essex. "It is difficult for us," he declared, "in this ancient forest of Theydon Bois—the very name of which carries us back to Norman days—here, in the heart of peaceful, law-abiding England, to comprehend that the whole state of Europe and of the world is moving steadily towards a climax which cannot be long delayed."

The climax to which Churchill referred was, of course, war. He warned his audience, many of whom were picnicking on the grass, that "ferocious passions" were boiling on the continent and that Nazi Germany had mobilized "fifteen hundred thousand soldiers upon a war footing." Time was running out, Churchill declared: England must hasten to rearm. There was a scattering of applause, there were a few boos and laughs, a few good-natured cries of "You tell 'em, Winnie!" Part of the crowd began to drift away to watch a nearby soccer match. Good old Winnie—or poor old Winnie, depending on your viewpoint—was harping on his favorite theme again, and it had become something of a bore over the years.

Indeed with many, perhaps most Englishmen, Churchill's oft-repeated and clamorous warnings about the inevitability of conflict had earned him the reputation of being a warmonger. But what could you expect? At sixty-four the old man was an unreconstructed, dyed-in-the-wool Victorian imperialist of the most militant variety. In his youth he'd marched with Kitchener to the conquest of the Sudan; later he'd fought in the Boer War, in which he'd been captured by the enemy and then made a sensational escape; and he'd reached the height of his career during the First World War, when, as First Lord of the Admiralty, he'd directed Britain's mighty fleets against the Kaiser's Germany. Hadn't his exceeding bellicosity during that struggle been responsible for the ill-conceived and foredoomed disaster of the Dardanelles campaign of 1916? As American historian Barbara Tuchman observed, Winston Churchill was like that biblical horse in the Book of Job who, smelling the battle far off, "paweth in the valley and saith among the trumpets, Ha, ha." Besides, the man was a political maverick. He'd started out a Conservative, then joined the Liberal Party, and now was a Conservative once again. His own party distrusted him and he'd spent many of the previous ten years out of office, an eccentric voice in the political wilderness.

But there are things to be learned in the wilderness, and as a private citizen Churchill kept himself very well informed about the military and political currents beneath the surface of European life that were leading to that climax of which he warned. And those currents swirled most dangerously in Germany.

From the consequences of defeat in World War I—national dismemberment, revolutionary chaos, social upheaval, and national embitterment; from older traditions of racism, militarism, and autocracy; above all from the ravages of the Great Depression of 1929–1933—a new kind of totalitarian political movement had come to power in Germany. Organized behind the banners of the Nazi party—a collection of cynical opportunists, militaristic adventurers, warped intellectuals, criminals, and thugs—the distressed German masses had given their allegiance to a powerfully charismatic, cunning, fanatical dictator named Adolf Hitler, whom Churchill very accurately described as "this monstrous embodiment of former shames and wrongs."

Hitler's program for Germany, Europe, and the world was by no means secret: Not only did he constantly proclaim it in public speeches, but he had written it all down in his political testament *Mein Kampf* (*My Battle*) for those who were willing to read. Germany was to become an absolute dictatorship in which no opposition—political, social, religious, intellectual—would be permitted. Every aspect of German life was to be organized, policed, and dedicated to the worship of the German state and its absolute leader. Germany was to rearm, to build a mighty and invincible war machine with which it would first "correct" the "unfair" provisions of the peace treaties of 1918, then conquer vast expanses of *Lebensraum* (living space) in Eastern Europe.

This campaign of conquest ought to enlist the cooperation of the western democracies because it would be conducted under the guise of a crusade against communism. If the democracies resisted this program it hardly mattered: They were weak, corrupt, decadent, and would be crushed. Underlying this ferocious plan were conceptions that could only be described as totally insane. For Hitler's ultimate aims were not only military and political, they were genocidal. Germans, he believed, were by nature and biological evolution the world's "master race," entitled to rule mankind. Certain "lesser breeds," such as the Latins, might be useful as slaves; but others, especially Jews, Slavs, and "coloreds" were to be ruthlessly exterminated. The eventual goal was to be a purification of the entire human species until it conformed to the white, blue-eyed, blond Teutonic "ideal."

Madness, no doubt. But did Hitler really mean it or was this simply election-winning demagoguery? Churchill decided he must see for himself. So, in 1933, a few months after Hitler came to power in Berlin, he made a trip to Germany as a private tourist. On this mission he was accompanied by an old friend and adviser, Frederick Lindemann, later Lord Cherwell, a thin, craggy-faced mathematician and scientist known as "the Prof" who maintained close contact with scientists throughout the world. For some time the Prof had been worried about German development of new weapons, especially some sort of atomic explosive of potentially earth-shattering power.

The two friends journeyed throughout Germany—to cities, towns, universities. They saw a nation inundated by hate propaganda where every means of expression had come under state control. They saw regiments of brown-shirted storm troopers marching through the streets to the pounding of war drums, their voices raised in hoarse shouts of *Sieg Heil!* and *Heil Hitler!* They saw children being organized into the paramilitary Hitler Youth organizations. And they saw all who opposed Hitler—trade unionists, Communists, liberals, Catholic and Protestant religious leaders, intellectuals, artists, some scientists—being carted off to certain death in so-called concentration camps. They saw too the beginning of Hitler's war of extermination against the Jews —the shattered shops, the burned-out synagogues, the looted homes, the mob-ravaged ghettos. Everywhere they found a nation hysterically dedicated to the antihuman, paranoid fantasies of a *Führer* (leader) who promised them world domination. Churchill and Lindemann returned to England absolutely convinced that Hitler meant what he said and with frightening evidence that he was marshalling the resources of Europe's mightiest industrial power to put his plans into effect.

Churchill and the Prof were not the only visitors to Germany that summer of 1933. A close friend of theirs, a remarkable Canadian inventor and industrialist named William Stephenson, made his own tour of inspection, but unlike Churchill and Lindemann he did not seek anonymity. On the contrary, he talked to German industrial, military, and political leaders on the highest level.

Stephenson, later Sir William Stephenson, had been born in 1896 in Winnipeg and had grown up on the great plains of western Canada. When the First World War broke out he immediately volunteered for the Canadian Royal Engineers and served in the grim trenches of the western front for a year before being invalided out, the victim of a German gas attack. Although he was proclaimed unfit for further military service, Stephenson wangled his way into the Royal Flying

Corps, the forerunner of the RAF, and as a fighter pilot shot down twenty-six German aircraft by 1918. But in July of that year his luck ran out. He was shot down and taken prisoner by the Germans. Within three months he escaped and made his way back to London, where he arrived just in time to join in the victory celebrations of November 11, 1918.

As a fighter pilot Stephenson had shown himself unusual even for that breed of daredevil; his flying reports were thoughtful, analytical, and advocated the application of scientific organizing principles to the air war. These reports found their way into the hands of Admiral Sir Reginald Hall, the head of MI-6, the "C" of that era. So impressed was Hall that after the war he made sure that Stephenson went through Oxford University and that he kept in unofficial touch with Britain's Secret Intelligence Service. But the young Canadian's career was only beginning, and it was to be played out on a global stage.

Stephenson's interests were immensely varied, but basically they involved the application of scientific discovery and inventions—many his own—to the burgeoning new industries that developed in the years after World War I. Always dedicated to flying, he served for a while as a test pilot, helped develop and finance new aircraft design, and found himself the owner of several large aircraft factories. Fascinated by radio and electronic communications, he helped found both the Canadian and British Broadcasting Corporations and, with his friend and employee, Charles Steinmetz, developed the first television system in 1922. He saw in film the potential for mass education as well as entertainment, and by the thirties his was the controlling influence in international film production outside Hollywood. By then a multimillionaire, Stephenson's investments in new processes and products extended his interests and his knowledge into industries from mining to steel, from shipping to automobile production. His corporations were international—and so were his connections. It was no wonder that when he visited Germany in 1933 all doors were open to him.

Of course the Germans had no way of knowing that this "businessman" had never cut his links to British Intelligence, or that he had long warned those British politicians who would listen of Germany's secret rearmament in defiance of the restrictions imposed in 1918. Anxious to exchange patents, German industrialists proudly showed Steinmetz their new tractor factories—while his experienced eye saw the machine tools for tank production. Hoping for his investment, Nazi aircraft manufacturers displayed their latest "commercial" planes—while he studied their poorly camouflaged designs for deadly fighters and bombers. And German military leaders indiscreetly boasted to him of how they were preparing a new kind of warfare—*Blitzkrieg* (lightning war)— in which swarms of dive bombers would act as aerial artillery working in conjunction with vast masses of tanks, self-propelled artillery, and armored personnel carriers. These highly mobile *Panzer* (tank) armies would thrust with swift brutality through an enemy's lines of defense. Speed—speed of concentration, speed of maneuver, speed of exploitation of a breakthrough—everything would depend on speed. But how would the German generals control these fast-moving, far-ranging armored columns and their air umbrellas of fighters and bombers? Through radio, which now, for the first time in history, made instantaneous communications possible. And if an enemy intercepted these communications? The German military experts smiled. Let them! Their new

codes were scientifically machine-produced and would
change daily or even hourly. They would prove impenetrable.

As Stephenson listened to the Nazi leaders and witnessed
the viciousness of life in Hitler's police state, he realized that
war was inevitable, and that this time it would not be merely
a war to preserve national interests nor even a war to save
civilization. It would be a war to save most of the human
race from the extermination planned for it. Nor would this
coming struggle be only or even primarily military. It would
be, above all, political: a battle for the minds and souls of
men. As he flew back to London, where he would discuss all
these matters with Churchill and Lindemann, William
Stephenson wondered whether the moral resources of the
West would prove strong enough to withstand the coming
onslaught.

As well he might. For rarely had the fiber of public life
been weaker in the democracies than it was during the "long
truce," as Churchill called it, between 1918 and 1939. It
wasn't that citizens of the Atlantic world were unaware of
the horrors being prepared for them beyond the Rhine; they
were simply too demoralized to face up to them. The catastrophic First World War and its aftermath had sapped the
vitality and eroded the values upon which democratic societies were founded.

Take the French, for example. They maintained what was
considered to be the world's most powerful standing army;
they had constructed an "impregnable" chain of underground fortifications known, after its designer, as the
Maginot Line along their border with Germany; they maintained mutual-security treaties with the small Central and
Eastern European nations, Austria, Czechoslovakia, Poland,

Europe after Versailles

Areas which changed ownership; which were
formed into new states, etc., as a result
of the Treaty of Versailles

Romania, which had come into existence with the peace treaties of 1919. But behind these impressive defense systems lay no *will* to fight. French public life was constantly stained by scandal and corruption; French politics were continually plagued by the squabblings and intrigues of Socialists, Monarchists, Communists, Fascists, and splintered Liberal parties. Public faith in the Third Republic and its free institutions was weak, the attitude of most citizens totally cynical. On only one matter were most Frenchmen united: France had lost nearly two million men—an entire generation—in the mud-filled trenches and moonscaped battlefields of World War I. It must never happen again. To prevent a recurrence of that tragedy the French people and their constantly changing governments would pay almost any price, for France itself could not survive another such bloodletting.

As for the English, they too had suffered grievously during the World War, losing nearly a million men, and they too were determined never again to be engulfed in such madness. After the guns fell silent on the Western Front in 1918, most Englishmen happily retired into their old attitude of "splendid isolation." After all, they still enjoyed the embrace of their vast Commonwealth of Nations and the world's most extensive empire. Why seek trouble in the endless quarrels of Europe? Besides, although the British Army and the RAF had been reduced to a pitiful, underequipped handful of men and officers, Britain was defended, as always, by the mighty if aging Royal Navy—still far and away the world's most powerful. And although the English people retained faith and confidence in their ancient freedoms and institutions, it seemed that they had become a nation of pacifists. When the Oxford Student Union adopted a resolution declaring that the youth of England should never again go forth to "die for King and Country," polls showed that most Englishmen agreed with them. "Peace at any price" was the motto that dominated British political life during the years between the wars.

The Americans had gone off to the First World War as to a crusade. They believed very sincerely that they were fighting to "make the world safe for democracy" in that "war to end all wars." Coming late to the battlefields, they had not suffered the grievous losses of the other combatants, but they were just as disillusioned by the peace that followed the fighting. The American president, Woodrow Wilson, a rigid idealist, had described a postwar world of freedom everywhere, self-determination for all peoples, open boundaries, free trade, and more, all of which was to be guarded by a League of Nations that would enforce eternal peace.

But Wilson's dreams fell afoul of European realities and American politics. The French, with their desperate quest for security, and the English, pursuing their balance of power policies, carved up Europe irrespective of self-determination and imposed a peace of utmost vengeance on defeated Germany. As for the League of Nations, it came into being all right, with headquarters in neutral Switzerland. But largely because the United States refused to join, it was soon reduced to an international debating society, powerless to either maintain peace or provide security for its members. Convinced they had been swindled by the idealists, Americans retired into isolationism and the selfish pursuit of that false prosperity that characterized the "Roaring Twenties." And since their shores, both east and west, were protected by huge and "impassable" oceans, they reduced their army and air force to minuscule proportions and sank most of the unfinished warships they'd built during the war. Americans were absolutely determined never again to become embroiled in European politics and quarrels.

If fear, disillusionment, cynicism, and pacifism undermined the will to resist aggression in the western democracies following World War I, there came upon them in 1929 a catastrophe which seemed to complete their demoralization. This was the agony of the Great Depression with its deflated stock exchanges, closed factories, mines, and mills, foreclosed farms, failed banks, bread lines, poverty, and mass unemployment. Amid these appalling conditions no western government was willing to "waste" scarce resources upon armaments. Defense budgets, already at a minimum, were cut to the vanishing point. And so heavy was the blow, so complete the economic ruin and social upheaval, so pervasive and endless the suffering, that many in America, Britain, and France lost faith in their free institutions. They began to turn to totalitarian solutions: fascism, as practiced by the swaggering Italian dictator Benito Mussolini; communism as established in the Soviet Union; and even Herr Hitler's mad brand of tyranny. To be sure, democratic solutions to the painful problems of the Great Depression were being sought and applied in Britain, France, and especially in the United States under the leadership of President Franklin D. Roosevelt. But the process was bitterly controversial, seemingly endless. When Nazi propagandists proclaimed the democracies weak, divided, decadent, and corrupt, they appeared to speak no more than the truth. When they boasted that Hitler's sick dreams represented "the wave of the future," many, even among their most determined opponents, feared they might be right.

Of course, the democracies were not Hitler's only potential enemies in Europe and the world. There was also the Soviet Union, from whose territory he planned to carve the new German empire, whose citizens he planned to exterminate, and whose communist system he continually denounced in the most bloodcurdling terms. So obvious were Nazi intentions toward Russia that many western statesmen clung to the hope that the two dictatorships would fall upon and destroy each other.

The Russians had been isolated from European affairs after the Bolshevik Revolution of 1917 and their subsequent surrender to the Germans in 1918. The newly established Union of Soviet Socialist Republics was the self-proclaimed archenemy of capitalist democracy; the French alliances in Eastern Europe were designed as much to prevent the spread of communism as to deter renewed German aggression. Believing themselves (correctly) to be surrounded by mortal enemies, Soviet leaders manipulated native communist parties abroad to keep capitalist countries off balance through propaganda, subversion, and constant radical agitation. After Lenin's death in 1924, dictatorial power in Russia passed into the hands of Josef Stalin, who announced that henceforth the Soviets would no longer await the millennium of worldwide Communist revolution but would instead concentrate on "building socialism in one country." What he meant by that phrase was the construction of a monolithic tyranny based on police terror, slave-labor camps, and total state control of economic and social life, for political life outside the rigid hierarchy of the Russian Communist party was simply not permitted.

As for the threat of Nazi aggression, Stalin did not at first believe in it. During the 1920's the Soviet Union had made secret agreements with the leaders of the Weimar Republic, permitting the German army and air force to build and test their new weapons and, through maneuvers, to try out their theories of *Blitzkrieg* on the vast Russian plains. In return the Germans built armament factories in Russia and shared their military secrets with the Red army. When Hitler came to power in 1933—partly because Stalin had instructed the large German Communist party not to oppose him—he was regarded as a passing phenomenon. "The road to a Communist Germany" Stalin declared, "lies through Hitler."

In 1935, when Nazi intentions became clearer to the autocrats in the Kremlin, Stalin embarked on a campaign to enlist the democracies in a united front against Fascist aggression. But there was little reason for western governments to ally themselves with their sworn enemy, even had they the will and the means. Then, in 1936, the Nazi intelligence agencies, animated by one of Hitler's young intellectual thugs, Reinhard Heydrich, concocted a brew of letters and documents that seemed to reveal a widespread anti-Stalinist conspiracy in the Red army. They cleverly served this forged poison to the suspicious Soviet dictator, who swallowed it whole. Within two years, through a series of bloody "purges," Stalin massacred fully half the officers of his armed forces, utterly destroying his own high command and effectively crippling Russian military power.

And the years ticked away like a time bomb. In 1931 Imperial Japan seized Manchuria from the divided and prostrate Chinese Republic. The League of Nations investigated and protested; Japan contemptuously left the League and that was that. In 1935 the Italian Fascist dictator, Benito Mussolini, sent his armies to the conquest of Ethiopia. There were protests and even halfhearted economic sanctions but again no real actions. In 1936 the Spanish

Civil War broke out. Italy and Germany sent vital military support to the Fascist rebels while Russia lent the Spanish Republic just enough help to keep it alive. Aside from organizing a fatuous "Nonintervention Committee," the western democracies did nothing and thereby doomed the Republic to eventual defeat. Later that same year Hitler ordered his army to reoccupy the German Rhineland, demilitarized since 1919 by the terms of the peace treaties. There were worried consultations between London and Paris, but in the end neither France nor Britain lifted a finger—and this despite the fact that, by heavily fortifying their western frontier, the Germans would now be able to prevent the French from marching to the aid of their Eastern European allies. In 1937 the Japanese embarked on the conquest of China in a brutal war they called an "incident," which was to continue for nearly ten years. Aside from sympathetic noises the democracies offered no aid to the Chinese. In February of 1938, now firmly allied to Mussolini, Hitler sent his army marching into neighboring Austria. Meeting no resistance from the feeble Austrian Republic, the Nazis joyfully proclaimed the *Anschluss* (Joining) of Austria to the Third Reich. To allay British and French fears, Hitler declared that he was, after all, only reuniting Germans and that universal peace was now at hand. On this occasion Winston Churchill told the House of Commons, "When Hitler began, Germany lay prostrate at the feet of the Allies. Hitler may yet see the day when what is left of Europe will be prostrate at the feet of the Germans." No one listened. Later that same year, during the summer of 1938, Hitler demanded, on threat of war, that Czechoslovakia cede to Germany the Sudetenland, her mountainous frontier territory in which three million Germans lived. The Czechs mobilized their army and prepared to fight. The Russians announced they would honor their mutual-defense treaty with Czechoslovakia provided France did the same. France ordered partial mobilization and looked to England for support. It seemed, as Churchill told his constituents in the "ancient forest of Theydon Bois" that August bank-holiday weekend, that the ticking time bomb must now go off.

But in the end it didn't. At the last moment, on September 29, 1938, British Prime Minister Neville Chamberlain and French Premier Édouard Daladier, both peace-loving and perhaps naive politicians, flew to a meeting with Hitler and Mussolini at Munich in Germany. There they abandoned the Czechs and accepted all of Hitler's demands. Chamberlain returned to London hopefully proclaiming "peace in our time." Hitler, he declared, was a man you could trust, a man you could do business with. The German *Führer* had given his solemn word that Germany had no more territorial ambitions in Europe. Churchill said, "We have sustained a great defeat without a war." Stalin drew his own conclusions.

Had Hitler, then, no determined enemies during the years of his bloodless conquests? He did, but they were lonely, isolated, rendered powerless by the political climate of the times. In the United States, President Franklin D. Roosevelt and some of his more intimate advisers recognized the growing Nazi threat and attempted to awaken Americans to the peril. FDR, beginning in 1935, made various speeches in which he called for a "quarantine of the aggressors" and warned Americans of their inescapable "rendezvous with destiny." Congress responded with neutrality legislation designed to keep America out of war and that effectively prevented any possible aid to Hitler's victims. Despite presidential warnings, Americans were determined to cling to isolationism, and on this one issue Roosevelt could not sway public opinion. If he attempted to push matters too far he risked electoral defeat or even impeachment.

Even inside Germany Hitler had dedicated enemies deeply hidden among members of the old aristocracy, the general staff, and the Nazi party itself. For it was obvious to some German leaders that *der Führer's* madness was propelling Germany toward war and ultimate disaster. Nurtured by Admiral Wilhelm Canaris, the chief of German Intelligence —and an old acquaintance from World War I days of his British counterpart, Colonel Menzies—the German resistance movement was known as the *schwarze Kapelle* (Black Orchestra) to those Nazi secret police officials who suspected its existence. The *schwarze Kapelle,* which included many of Germany's top generals and field marshals, planned Hitler's overthrow whenever he should meet really determined Allied resistance. Agents from the German general staff warned the English and French governments before each of Hitler's aggressions, expecting that the western powers would then stand up to the Nazis and provide the excuse upon which the German conspirators could act. But, as we have seen, from 1933 to 1939, the Allies preferred to appease Hitler, and the *schwarze Kapelle's* hour never came.

To those who did not live through the muddled era of appeasement or the disasters of the Second World War that followed, all of this must seem incredible. Couldn't people see what was so plainly written on the wind? Couldn't they realize that war was imminent and that when it came it would be France and England against Germany, Italy, and probably Japan? And even if no one could read Stalin's mind, was it not perfectly obvious that Hitler would sooner or later attack Russia? As for the United States, couldn't

Americans see from the very beginning that their only salvation lay with the Allies?

Unfortunately it is not given to most of us to see very far or very deeply into the future, and for those few who are able to do so, history holds high honors. For the rest of us, as the American philosopher George Santayana long ago pointed out, "those who will not learn history are condemned to repeat it."

But although such prophets of those days as Churchill were, for a while, without honor in their own countries, and most people everywhere blinded themselves to what lay ahead, that generation of freedom-loving people nevertheless deserves our respect and gratitude, for by their exertions and their sacrifices they defeated the deadliest foe that ever arose against humanity, and bought us all a little more time to make the world safe for our own species.

Of course, the great struggles and battles of World War II have been endlessly detailed; the swift German conquest of Europe and then of most of Russia; the seesaw fighting between the English and Germans in North Africa; the savage, lonely war that was waged on and beneath the icy waters of the North Atlantic; Japan's tide of conquest in the Far East and the Allied and Russian counterattacks that drove back and eventually crushed the aggressors. Such names as Stalingrad, El Alamein, Midway, Pearl Harbor, Bataan, D-Day, the Bulge, Sicily, Anzio, and Iwo Jima are familiar to all of us. They were among the great, open battles of the war.

But they were not the only battles. For behind the flaming fronts on which millions of men fought and died, another, secret war took place. It was a war of lonely individuals against the mighty German war machine, a war in which men, women, and even children were combatants, a war of unparalleled savagery, of cunning duplicity and deception, a war that never made the headlines and of which, until very recently, almost nothing was known. Yet this secret war of spies and counterspies, of deceiving whispers, of double-crossings and assassinations, of sleight-of-hand, torture, suicide, and ruthless sacrifice, made all the famous victories possible.

This hidden war, with its spy agents and underground armies, was directed for the most part by professionals, but it was fought by many thousands of ordinary individual citizens who volunteered for the purpose. These men and women were not motivated by greed; the reward of the spy was often torture and death, not money. They were not motivated by a longing for glory; their work was secret and would, they knew, be kept secret for decades. They did not desire martyrdom; they all hoped they would survive their lonely missions despite the terrible odds against them. What moved them to take awesome risks, endure indescribable terror and pain, suffer death, and often enough find unmarked graves were ideals. They believed in freedom, in liberty, in the right of all human beings to share the earth together; they believed in humanity. Were they then soft-hearted, unrealistic, foolish? If so, why were they such terrible and deadly-effective foes of the warlords, mass murderers, and antihuman politicians they finally destroyed?

They are mostly gone now, killed in the struggle or dead in the decades since. Their work was shrouded in secrecy for thirty years after the war, and even now much of it remains unknown. We know, and will know, very little about them as people. Their faces have faded from memory; their names, even their code names, have been forgotten. Researchers and historians have recently rescued a few from the dusty oblivion of long-sealed files. We know something now of the individuals behind such code names as "Cynthia," "Madeleine," "Prosper," "Major Martin," and a handful of others. They were not extraordinary people, but they accomplished extraordinary things. During the Second World War almost all the secret agents were amateurs. They were drawn from all walks and conditions of life. There was no "spy personality," no common collection of characteristics about them. Indeed, they were notably diverse in everything except dedication.

Sometimes their dedication was exploited without their knowledge; sometimes they were used and sacrificed as pawns in a master game of which they were completely unaware. For the spy masters in London and Washington directed their secret armies with utmost ruthlessness. The end —total victory over the enemy—justified in their minds any and all means. In a later, calmer time one may question some of those means, especially when they involved the knowing sacrifice of individual agents, networks of agents, entire armies, large civilian populations. But the judgment of history must always be weighed on the scale of possible alternatives, and the alternative to Allied victory in the secret war would surely have been a worldwide holocaust beside which even the tragedy of European Jewry would have paled.

As we explore the story of the secret war against Hitler, it will become obvious that the enemies of freedom, with a very few exceptions, lost all the important intelligence battles. Time and again they were outwitted and duped by Allied deceptions and schemes; they were never to realize that their most secret plans and orders were being "read" by Allied cryptographers almost as soon as they were issued;

they rarely guessed that their own agents had been "turned" against them; they had but little success competing with Allied propagandists for the allegiance of neutral people. Why?

The first and most obvious reason is that intelligence operations depend on just that: intelligence. But the Nazi and Fascist ideologies suspected and condemned human reason. Leading German and Italian intellectuals, scientists, and technicians, teachers, artists, writers—all those of inquiring and imaginative mind—had either been forced into flight or murdered in concentration camps long before the war began. And, of course, the savage Nazi occupation forces could by no means enlist the help of such people in conquered lands; on the contrary, "conquered" men and women of learning and wit worked actively against them. As for the professional German Intelligence services, these were, as we shall see, directed against the Nazi warlords by leaders who were convinced that Hitler was leading Germany to ruin. There were, of course, not a few Nazi Intelligence agents who were both daring and cunning, but their activities were based almost entirely upon terror—the extraction of information through torture, the gaining of civilian "cooperation" through the threat of massacre, the use of brute force in place of reason itself. The very essence of the Nazi threat lay in its intention to turn humans into robots, its dependence on the mechanization of human life, its arrogant appraisal of all enemies as subhuman. But robots do not make good intelligence agents, machines cannot compete with human wit, and arrogance blinds even cunning men to their own vulnerability.

Did Churchill, Lindemann, and William Stephenson foresee all this from the very first? They foresaw much of it. They knew at least that they would be fighting a war of individuals against a monolithic, heavily-armed, terroristic state. And in England as early as 1933 they began recruiting intellectuals, scientists, certain military and naval officers, and members of the intelligence services into informal "discussion groups," "scientific societies," and "literary clubs" whose real purpose was to devise new and unorthodox methods of meeting the Nazi threat. They had to operate with almost no money and in the deepest secrecy from their own government, whose hidebound bureaucracy and fatuous leadership they simply could not trust. Calling themselves the Baker Street Irregulars—after the gang of street urchins who helped Sherlock Holmes solve some of his mysteries, these dedicated amateurs and rebellious professionals explored such matters as guerrilla tactics, economic warfare, industrial sabotage, assassination, terrorism, propaganda— all the means, both fair and foul, by which an unarmed nation might hope to defend itself against a mighty war machine. They also kept a close watch on progress in atomic physics and, with increasing urgency, sought some means to penetrate Enigma. . . .

The War Diary

September 1, 1939/Germany invades Poland.

September 3, 1939/Britain and France declare war on Germany.

September 20, 1939/Russian forces invade Poland from the east.

September 29, 1939/German and Russian forces divide conquered Poland.

November 30, 1939/Russian forces attack Finland.

April 9, 1940/German forces overrun Denmark and invade Norway.

April 10, 1940/Finland accepts Soviet peace terms. Soviet forces occupy Latvia, Lithuania, and Estonia.

April 30, 1940/German conquest of Norway complete.

May 8, 1940/Winston Churchill becomes British prime minister.

THE ORACLE OF BLETCHLEY   2

The beginning of every war is
like opening a door into a dark room.
One never knows what is hidden in the darkness.

ADOLF HITLER

Colonel Colin McVeagh Gubbins, Royal Artillery, was
known as one of the best-dressed men in London. Always
impeccably turned out, he generally sported a red carnation
in his buttonhole and invariably carried kidskin gloves. He
was of medium height, trimly muscled, of florid complexion,
and conducted himself in that vague if hearty manner typical
of middle-aged artillery officers whose brains have long since
been stunned by the roaring of their guns. Those who knew
him thought of him as a "chap with no particular talents and
some sort of desk job in the War Office"—one of those rigid,
old-line officers planning to fight the Second World War as
they had fought the First. And if Gubbins's acquaintances
were mistaken in this assessment, they could hardly be
blamed, for he was an excellent actor.

Yet behind Gubbins's bluff-but-amiable manner lurked a highly original mind and the spirit of an old-time highway-man. A master of several Slavonic languages, he had traveled extensively. And far from holding orthodox military views, he had written several instruction manuals for guerrilla fighting. His books, *The Art of Guerrilla Warfare*, *Partisan Leader's Guide*, and *The Housewife's ABC of Home-Made Explosives*, were hair-raising handbooks for savage, unconventional warfare, produced in defiance of a War Office that greeted with amusement his assertion in 1938 that "The coming war with Germany will have to be fought by irregular or guerrilla forces at all possible points."

Of course, unknown to friends, acquaintances, and fellow officers, Colonel Gubbins was a high-ranking member of MI-6—and unknown to many members of that intelligence agency, he was also among those gifted amateurs and professionals Stephenson and Churchill had recruited for the Baker Street Irregulars. Not that his unofficial activities were hidden from Colonel Menzies, the Chief of MI-6; nothing was hidden from Menzies. But much was hidden from the British government by Menzies, Gubbins, and other professional intelligence officers who were, after all, employed by that government. The problem was that they simply could not trust appeasement-minded politicians and ministers, even at the highest level, to guard their secrets. This apparent conflict of loyalties was resolved in their own minds by a medieval twist of the unwritten British constitution, which, since the days of Elizabeth I, provided that the higher officers of English intelligence services should be confirmed in their jobs by the Crown itself. Their positions were held to be "within the gift of the Monarch." So long as their activities helped to defend the interests of the king and his sub-jects, they did not feel they were committing treason by deceiving and circumventing the transient governments of the day.

And another such deception was brewing during the summer of 1939; it had to do with Enigma. The Polish engineer X who'd been interviewed by Knox and Turing a year earlier had been, as planned, spirited from Warsaw to France. There, as he'd promised, he recreated from memory a complete Enigma machine of the type manufactured in the Berlin factory where he'd been employed. It was, according to Knox, Turing, and other members of the Golf, Cheese, and Chess Society, a "marvel of imitative engineering." There was just one difficulty: X's version of Enigma was now hope-lessly out of date. Newer, much more complex models of the German coding device were being produced at a factory on the Czech border, and if British cryptanalysts were to pene-trate its secrets, it was now urgent that they study this newer model—urgent because war was now very close.

Having convinced British Prime Minister Neville Chamber-lain at Munich that his seizure of the Czech Sudetenland was his last territorial ambition and that henceforth Europe would enjoy eternal peace and stability, Hitler contemptu-ously broke his word when, six months later, on March 15, 1939, he sent his armies over the Czech borders to occupy the remainder of that unhappy country. A wave of outrage in England forced even the appeasement-minded Chamberlain to change his policy. The British prime minister hastened to issue a series of guarantees to the remaining countries of Eastern Europe that Britain would defend them from Nazi aggression. How Britain was to accomplish this in its unarmed condition was not explained. No matter, the die was cast, and any further German encroachments would mean war.

Further encroachments were precisely what Hitler had in mind. His next victim was to be Poland, where, he ranted, millions of "mistreated" Germans were longing for the day when they could be reunited with their Fatherland. Having successfully bluffed Britain and France for six years, *der Führer* was fairly sure he could bluff them again: They would not really fight over Poland. And if they did it hardly mattered; the German *Blitzkrieg* would quickly annihilate all enemies. And while the war drums beat in Berlin, Hitler prepared yet another stunning surprise for the western democracies—his nonaggression pact with the Soviet Union, which was signed in Moscow on August 23, 1939. Stalin, convinced that the West would not and could not stand up to Hitler, was willing enough to mend fences with the Nazi dictator, especially since secret provisions of the treaty gave Russia a free hand to exploit her own territorial ambitions in Eastern Europe. At a stroke the last possible deterrent to German aggression was thus removed.

It was after Chamberlain's guarantee to Poland, early in 1939, that Menzies sent Colonel Gubbins and a team of assistants to Warsaw. Their mission, he explained to the government, would be to coordinate British and Polish intelligence activities in the event of war. He did not tell his political superiors that Gubbins's real aim was, by hook or by crook, to get hold of a new production model of Enigma. By both hook and crook, with the help of Polish Intelligence, this was done in mid-August.

The Germans, it seemed, were sending new Enigma machines to their front-line units along the Polish border in preparation for the coming assault. A Polish spy reported that such a delivery would be made by truck to a German outpost in Danzig. Since both German and Polish forces policed this supposedly free city on the Baltic, it was no problem to set a trap. As the German truck rumbled through the night along a deserted stretch of road, it was suddenly rammed broadside by a heavy oil tanker. The German driver was killed instantly on impact and the truck was overturned. Several men leaped from the tanker's cab, quickly removed the Enigma machine from the wreckage, replaced it with charred bits of coils, wires, metal, and wood, then set fire to the truck. The entire incident was over in three minutes and the oil tanker vanished into the night. Later, German investigators were perfectly satisfied that their Enigma had been consumed in the flames of this unfortunate accident.

The following day, at Warsaw's Hotel Bristol, where Colonel Gubbins was staying, a mix-up occurred with some luggage. It seemed that the colonel's large, old-fashioned leather traveling bag, which had been left in the lobby with several other suitcases, had disappeared. In its place had been left an identical bag containing clothing and books. The mistake was obviously unintentional. As soon as whoever had taken Gubbins's bag opened it he'd realized his error and returned it to the hotel, so the colonel made no complaint.

Eight hours later Colonel Gubbins's missing bag turned up in London. It was carried by a small, wiry, middle-aged man named Alastair Denniston, one of Britain's leading cryptanalysts. On instructions from Colonel Menzies, Denniston took the bag to the little town of Bletchley, some fifty miles north of the British capital. There, in the pretentious dining room of a huge, ugly red-brick Victorian mansion known as

Bletchley Hall—the former property of a businessman who'd lost his country estate to the government for failure to pay taxes—the bag was opened. It contained the German Enigma captured in Danzig. Now Knox, Turing, and the other experts of the Golf, Cheese, and Chess Society, all of whom had been transferred to Bletchley from London some months earlier, had the material they needed.

And none too soon. Barely a week after Enigma's arrival at Bletchley, Hitler's powerful armies crashed into Poland and the Second World War began. It took the German *Panzer* divisions a mere twenty days to reach Warsaw while the Russians, in accordance with secret provisions of their pact with the Nazis, seized Poland's eastern provinces. Colonel Gubbins gathered together his British team of agents and every Pole who knew anything at all about Enigma and led them on a trek through the mountains into neutral Romania. From there they made their way to France. The Nazi counterintelligence teams found no evidence in conquered Poland that their enemies had ever even heard of Enigma.

Now, with Britain at war—and fearfully unprepared for it—the penetration of German Enigma codes became a matter of vital urgency. It was to be accomplished through Alan Turing's invention of a universal machine that would "better appreciate" sonnets written by another machine. This Turing engine, as it was sometimes called—it was also referred to as the Bomb or Colossus—was painstakingly constructed over a period of months during 1939 by the British Tabulating Company, but it was not a calculating machine. Nor was it a computer, for which the technology did not then exist. In fact, it defied description. It was a data-processing machine about eight feet high, eight feet wide at the base, and several yards long—shaped, fittingly enough, like an old-fashioned keyhole. When it operated it emitted the sound of thousands of knitting needles clicking together. Certain elements of the Turing engine remain secret to this day. For example, it was obviously not enough for it to merely simulate Enigma and then try all possible combinations to decipher a message; even today no computer could run through 3×10^{18} possible combinations in a short enough time to make the information useful. We knew only that its secret lay in the wiring of its rotors, which "sought to imitate" the electric circuits of Enigma. Furthermore, the machine seemed to improve its own performance as more and more data was fed into it: It was self-educating.

The data consumed by the Turing engine were intercepts of German Enigma radio traffic. A forest of tall antennae soon grew at Bletchley—explained to the curious as a British Broadcasting Corporation monitoring center, which gathered wireless whispers from all over Europe. But this was not the only material available. Many radio intercepts came from the United States.

As early as 1935 U.S. cryptanalysts—a small, under-equipped, underfinanced team headed by William Friedman, whose activities were frowned upon as "ungentlemanly" by the State Department—had realized that Japan, too, was employing Enigma for her diplomatic and naval codes. Their attack on the Japanese Enigma paralleled British efforts, though the machine they developed, code-named Magic, was based on different—and still secret—principles. But as war erupted in Europe, Magic was becoming operational. It had the advantage of being portable enough to be carried on larger naval vessels—and the consequent disadvantage of possibly falling into enemy hands in battle. But although American and British cryptanalysts were tackling the same problems at the same time, they worked in absolute isolation from each other. American neutrality laws forbade the exchange of intelligence information with any other nation, while Britain's MI-6 was reluctant on its part to reveal secrets that might be accidentally leaked to the Germans. Yet, while not revealing the existence of Magic, the Americans, by secret directive of President Roosevelt, made available to Britain the flow of Japanese Enigma radio intercepts gathered on the vast American Mid-Pacific Radio Net, which spread from Alaska to Samoa.

This entire question of security that kept British and American cryptanalysts from pooling information and resources was vexatious but vital. Should the Germans discover that their Enigma traffic was being decoded they would simply and immediately shift to an entirely different system that might take years or forever to penetrate. And discovery could come in many ways—through spies, through leaks or careless talk on the part of the hundreds of civilians employed at Bletchley, through the capture of documents in battle, and most probably through German analysis of British activities. If the English appeared to have advance information of German plans, and *no other explanation* could be accepted, the Nazis would know that Enigma was no longer secure.

Colonel Menzies attacked this problem with energy and imagination. All information emanating from Bletchley was code-named Ultra, after the British admirals' code used at the battle of Trafalgar, and access to Ultra was restricted to the tiniest handful of individuals on a strict need-to-know basis. As for German spies, the two dozen or so operating in Britain were rounded up by MI-5 (Counterintelligence) and Scotland Yard within a few days of the outbreak of war.

Security among the civilians at Bletchley presented a different kind of problem. By late 1939 Bletchley Park was dotted with Nissen huts (one of which contained the Turing engine), in which hundreds of people worked night and day analyzing, translating, computing the great flow of Enigma traffic. With few exceptions these were not military or intelligence personnel but brilliant amateurs—mathematicians, logicians, chess masters, linguists—recruited from academic circles, unused to discipline, unimpressed by rank, title, or authority. There was always the threat, of course, of Britain's fearsome Official Secrets Act, which prescribed death as the ultimate deterrent to loose tongues, but this threat was never needed. Patriotism, common sense, and, above all, dedication to their work kept the inhabitants of Bletchley from revealing the slightest hint of Ultra, not only during the war, but for thirty years afterward.

As for the possibility of the Germans capturing Ultra documents in battle, there was a simple solution: There would be no such documents. Ultra information needed by British commanders in the field would be relayed to them by word of mouth. For this purpose Menzies organized a group of two-man teams to be attached only to the highest British field headquarters. These teams would receive Ultra messages by radio from London (coded, of course) and would transmit the information verbally to the British commander. The commander, except for a few of the highest-ranking officers, had no real idea of the source of this material—only that it could be relied upon. The equipment used by the teams, usually carried in a truck or trailer, could be easily destroyed in an emergency, while the teams themselves were prepared to commit suicide to avoid capture.

There remained the possibility of German analysis, for the

Nazis might deduce the breaking of their codes through the effectiveness of British countermeasures. For this reason two decisions were made: first of all, that any Ultra information must always be disguised as having come from some other source, such as spies, German traitors, the capture of German documents, neutral sources, indiscretions among Nazi personnel, reconnaissance of some sort; and second, if no such phony source could be persuasively trumped up, then Ultra information simply *could not be used.* This last decision was to have bitter and tragic consequences on more than one occasion, as we shall see.

And while the cryptanalysts at Bletchley labored furiously to make Ultra possible, a strange stalemate settled over the European battlefields, which were confined, now that Poland was conquered, to the French-German border. French soldiers huddled in their Maginot Line, German troops in their Siegfried Line, facing each other but rarely firing a shot in anger. The small British Expeditionary Force that took position along the neutral Belgian border occupied itself with athletics and routine military drill. At sea the Royal Navy, once again under the command of Winston Churchill—reappointed to his old post as First Lord of the Admiralty—vigorously pursued and sank German surface raiders while Nazi U-boats torpedoed a few Allied cargo and passenger vessels, but for six months following the fall of Warsaw so little military action took place anywhere that people referred to the conflict as "the phony war" or the *Sitzkrieg.* Only in the east, where Russia gobbled up the small Baltic nations of Lithuania, Latvia, and Estonia and attacked Finland, was there any action. Why?

Because despite everything the leaders of Britain and France still hoped for peace! If no large battles were fought, if no important casualties were suffered or inflicted, it might still be possible to reach some understanding with Nazi Germany, and then perhaps Hitler would finally turn his mighty war machine to the east against Russia, still his "natural" enemy despite the Nazi-Soviet pact. British delusions on this subject were carefully fostered by the Nazis. Swedish businessman Birger Dahlerus flew back and forth between London and Berlin by way of Stockholm all through the winter of 1939–1940 as the "personal representative" of *Luftwaffe* Chief Hermann Göring. Dahlerus's message to the English government was, essentially, "Sit still, do nothing violent, and there is still a good hope that Hitler will relent or even be overthrown; peace is still possible." So effective was this propaganda ploy with Chamberlain and certain of his advisers that the Royal Air Force was forbidden to bomb German targets.

But as the eerie winter of *Sitzkrieg* began to warm into spring, the first faint signs appeared that the period of phony war was drawing to an end. The signs were picked up at Bletchley—not through the Turing engine, which had yet to break its first Enigma codes, but through the forest of radio antennae surrounding Bletchley Park. These began to intercept an increasingly heavy flow of Nazi radio messages to and from military units, like an increase of sulfur in the air before a volcanic explosion. The Germans were concentrating their strength but not along the western front; the Nazi monster seemed to be turning its gaze northward, toward Scandinavia. Only a handful of men in Britain knew why this was so, among them First Lord of the Admiralty Winston Churchill and William Stephenson.

Nazi intelligence agents in Sweden began to suspect a British plot as soon as Stephenson arrived in Stockholm in

December 1939. True, the English businessman owned important commercial and industrial interests throughout Scandinavia and it might be that his visit was perfectly innocent. On the other hand Stephenson seemed to be spending entirely too much time with Axel Johnson, a Swedish industrialist with major holdings in Swedish iron-ore mines who also owned the railroad that brought the ore to Stockholm and the port facilities through which it was shipped—almost entirely—to Germany. Without the very high-grade iron ore provided by Johnson's mines, certain high-grade steels, vital to the German war effort, could no longer be produced. Needless to say, the Nazis kept a close watch on Stephenson's activities in Stockholm.

Their diligence was rewarded when German agents discovered that the Canadian businessman was receiving a steady flow of small parcels smuggled in from England. One of these parcels was intercepted and opened. It contained plastic explosive. Suddenly the plot became clear: Stephenson, in collaboration with his old friend Johnson, was preparing to blow up the port facilities through which that vital iron ore was shipped to Germany! Putting a stop to this British scheme was quite simple: The German Ambassador in Stockholm simply exposed the entire operation to the Swedish government. Sweden's King Gustav V angrily demanded that the English "halt this madness," and when Chamberlain found out what was afoot he ordered the operation canceled at once, declaring it to be "an unprecedented violation of international law." Having thus crippled the British plot, Nazi agents in Sweden took little further interest in William Stephenson—obviously a bungling amateur at intelligence operations.

Which was precisely what Stephenson had planned when

he made sure the Nazis would intercept that parcel of plastic explosive. Now, no longer under German surveillance, he simply vanished. Traveling with false papers and under a different name, he made his way north toward the arctic, crossed over into Norway, and, in the frozen Norwegian port of Narvik, secretly met with Professor Leif Tronstad, a Norwegian chemical engineer who happened to be very familiar with the layout of the Norsk Hydroelectric Plant near the town of Vemork. It was for this meeting that the entire elaborate Swedish mission had been mounted in the first place. Norsk Hydro was of great interest to Stephenson, Churchill, Lindemann, and other British scientists because it was the only plant in Europe where heavy water, deuterium oxide, was produced.

Heavy water—H_2O with an added molecule of hydrogen —was essential to atomic research in those days; it was used in experimental atomic piles as a moderator to control chain reactions, much as graphite rods were later used in atomic power plants. And Germany's giant chemical trust, I. G. Farben Industries, bought *all* of Norsk Hydro's output. British physicists knew the high quality of German research in this field, and the implications were terrifying: terrifying because in the last years of peace, scientists everywhere—from Columbia University to the California Institute of Technology, from Cambridge to Copenhagen—had already crossed over the threshold of the atomic age. They knew that sustained and controlled atomic chain reactions were possible and they knew that their theories were advanced enough to be turned into hardware—bombs that would be of awesome power. Much, of course, remained to be done. Years of effort and the labor of many thousands of individuals lay ahead, but the essential problems involved with the release of atomic power had been solved. With the coming of war, research in this field became a race between Allied and German scientists. Having received, in 1939, a letter from Albert Einstein warning him about the implications of atomic research, President Roosevelt had formed a secret committee of scientists to pursue the matter with secret government financing; in Britain Churchill had formed the British Uranium Committee for the same reason. But while British and American scientists worked at fever pace, it was essential to cripple similar German research. And this was what Stephenson wanted to discuss with Professor Tronstad.

There were, Stephenson explained to Tronstad, three ways of interrupting heavy-water shipments to Germany. The British could, through mining or direct naval action, sink the freighters that carried the stuff down Norwegian coastal waters to German ports, but this would involve so blatant a violation of Norwegian neutrality that the Germans might be prompted to intervene directly against Norway. Or British agents might somehow blow up the Norsk Hydro plant itself, but again, this would violate Norwegian neutrality, and besides, the Norwegian government would not take kindly to such sabotage. Finally, Tronstad himself, with a few friends, might neutralize the heavy water when it was ready for shipment by merely adding a small quantity of cod liver oil. This would make the fluid useless as a moderator, but this solution would be only a short-term measure. If the Germans should, for any reason, invade Norway and capture Norsk Hydro, then complete and detailed plans of the plant and its installations might one day be vital to British Intelligence. Would Professor Tronstad turn over those plans? The Professor would—and did. On a moonless night a few days later, his briefcase bulging with the complete blueprints of

Norsk Hydro, Stephenson rowed out into the harbor of Narvik. There he was picked up by a British submarine, which carried him back to England.

A brilliantly deceptive mission brilliantly carried out. But the problem of how to stop the flow of heavy water from Norway to Germany remained unresolved. The First Lord of the Admiralty pondered the question and finally, as was his way, opted for direct action. Norwegian coastal waters would be mined, and British submarines and destroyers would put an end to traffic with Germany. If this flagrant violation of Norwegian neutrality provoked the Germans, that could not be helped: The matter was far too important for any halfway measures. As for the timorous Chamberlain and his supporters, they would be told only that the Royal Navy was stopping the shipment of Norwegian iron ore to Germany.

When British submarines and destroyers began sinking German freighters in Norwegian coastal waters, the Germans were indeed provoked—which explained that heavy German radio traffic picked up by the listeners at Bletchley. . . .

When the Nazis struck, they struck suddenly, swiftly, and hard. On April 9, 1940, German troops overran Denmark and simultaneously began a sea and airborne invasion of Norway. When the Royal Navy attempted to intervene, it was driven off with heavy losses by packs of U-boats and by masses of *Luftwaffe* bombers, demonstrating for the first time in World War II the vulnerability of surface warships to air attack. Small British expeditionary forces landing belatedly on the Norwegian coast were soon driven back into the sea, the Norwegian army was quickly disposed of, and within a few weeks, Norway was completely conquered. But some Norwegians escaped to Britain, among them the Norwegian royal family, much of the Norwegian government, and certain key Norwegian scientists and technicians—including a certain Professor Leif Tronstad, formerly employed by Norsk Hydro.

The German conquest of Denmark and Norway had one good result: It toppled the British government of Neville Chamberlain and his appeasement-minded supporters. With the terrible words of Oliver Cromwell hurled at him in Parliament ("You have sat here too long for any good you have done! Begone! In the name of God, go!"), Chamberlain resigned as prime minister, and Winston Churchill, the political maverick, the outcast, the "warmonger," took his place.

Now all those informal, secret "committees," "societies," and "discussion groups" recruited and formed by Lindemann and Stephenson since the early thirties would enjoy the official blessing, protection, and support of His Majesty's Government. The Baker Street Irregulars were suddenly quite regular and perfectly free to wage their secret war against Germany "by means neither diplomatic nor military," as Churchill delicately put it.

And in those first days of May 1940, while the new prime minister was still organizing his cabinet, Colonel Menzies appeared one day at 10 Downing Street to hand-deliver a few slips of paper. The messages on them were of little importance—details about the transfer of certain *Luftwaffe* personnel, German army supply allocations to units in Denmark, and the like. Nevertheless, these little strips of paper were momentous, for they were the first Ultra messages. The Turing engine at Bletchley had begun to penetrate Enigma, and as it practiced its imitation of Enigma's deadly sonnets, it would grow in accuracy and efficiency. The oracle of Bletchley had started to speak—haltingly, stutteringly at first, but with a voice that would soon acquire decisive authority. And just in time, for the *Sitzkrieg* had ended and Hitler was about to launch real war upon France and Britain.

The War Diary

May 10, 1940/German forces invade Holland, Belgium, and France.

May 15, 1940/German conquest of Holland completed.

May 28, 1940/Belgium surrenders to Germany. British and French forces trapped at Dunkirk.

May 29–June 4, 1940/340,000 British and French troops evacuated to England from Dunkirk.

June 10, 1940/Italy declares war on Britain and France.

June 14, 1940/German troops enter Paris.

June 20, 1940/France surrenders to Germany. A French government under the leadership of Marshal Henri Pétain is established at Vichy.

June 30, 1940/Congress votes funds for FDR's "two-ocean navy."

July 3, 1940/The Royal Navy cripples Vichy French fleet units in North Africa to prevent their falling under German control.

August 2, 1940/The German air force begins full-scale attack on the RAF for air mastery over England.

September 7, 1940/The German air force commences night bombing of English cities.

November 5, 1940/Congress passes Selective Service Act establishing first peacetime American draftee army in history.

November 11, 1940/Franklin D. Roosevelt elected to a third term.

THE AMERICAN CONNECTION 3

If Britain should go down, all of us
in all the Americas would be living
at the point of a gun, a gun loaded
with explosive bullets . . .

FRANKLIN D. ROOSEVELT

On the very day, May 10, 1940, that Churchill officially
assumed his duties as prime minister, Hitler's forces struck
at Holland and Belgium with savage, overwhelming strength.
The Dutch held out just four days; then, with Rotterdam
burning from *Luftwaffe* bombings and the Dutch army
scattered, the Dutch government was forced to flee the
country to safety in England. In Belgium, German forces
advanced more slowly, as planned, while the British Expeditionary Force and French armies rushed forward to
stop the Nazi tide as far east in Belgium as possible. When
sufficient Allied troops had thus been sucked into the trap,
the German general staff, on May 14, unleashed a huge
armored force of five *Panzer* and ten motorized divisions to
crash through the weakly held Ardennes Forest, skirting the

Maginot Line and then driving north to the English Channel; the Allied forces in Belgium were thus cut off and surrounded. It was just as the German generals had boasted to William Stephenson in 1933: Preceded by Stuka dive-bombers screaming down out of the sky, and by waves of fighters and fighter-bombers, the huge mass of swift-moving Nazi armor destroyed everything in its path; advance German elements reached Abbeville on the Channel in just six days. Now all the Germans had to do was to drive northeastward along the Channel coast, capture the French and Belgian Channel ports to cut off any possible escape by sea, and then destroy the hapless Allied armies at their leisure.

This the Germans failed to do—for reasons that still elude historians. On direct orders from Hitler the Nazi *Panzer* divisions were halted before they completed their coastal drive, leaving the French Channel port of Dunkirk open to the British and French. It is said that Hermann Göring, anxious to secure glory for his *Luftwaffe,* persuaded *der Führer* that his air forces alone could batter the trapped armies into surrendering; it is said that Hitler was alarmed by the rate of mechanical breakdown suffered by his armored divisions in their swift advance; it is said that Hitler, still hoping for eventual peace with England, decided not to inflict upon British forces a total, humiliating defeat. Whatever the reason, the trapped Allies were given a few days breathing space.

Ultra had intercepted and decoded Hitler's personal halt order to the German commanders and the information was rushed to the British commander, Lord Gort. But Ultra was still new, its value uncertain. Lord Gort's decision to immediately evacuate as many troops as possible from Dunkirk was prompted not by Ultra dispatches but by the collapse of the Belgian army on his left flank and Belgium's subsequent surrender to the Germans. On the other hand, the Royal Navy, emboldened by the Ultra intercept, hastened preparations for Operation Dynamo, the immense fleet of naval, merchant, and private ships—everything from destroyers to freighters, from ferryboats to yachts—which by June 4 had evacuated no less than 338,326 British and French troops to safety in England. Losses were severe, but since the Royal Navy controlled the Narrow Seas and the RAF held the *Luftwaffe* at bay while the German armies were restrained by Hitler's personal order until it was too late for them to seize their prey, the "Miracle of Dunkirk" came to pass.

But while his countrymen and freemen everywhere rejoiced at the deliverance of Dunkirk, Winston Churchill noted that "wars are not won by evacuations." In grim fact, although the British Expeditionary Force and many French troops had been saved from capture, they had had to leave almost all their arms and equipment behind on the flaming Dunkirk beaches. Many returned to England without even their rifles. And this was the only fully trained and decently equipped army Britain could field. The English home islands were, by land at least, now almost entirely defenseless against a German invasion. But if he had little else to hurl at the Nazis, Churchill had defiance. On the same day, June 4, that the last of the defeated British Expeditionary Force found safety in English ports, he rose in Parliament to declare:

> *Even though large tracts of Europe and many old and famous states have fallen or may fall into the grip of the Gestapo and all the odious apparatus of Nazi rule, we shall not flag or fail . . . we shall fight on the beaches, we*

shall fight on the landing grounds, we shall fight in the fields and in the streets, we shall fight in the hills; we shall never surrender, and even if, which I do not for a moment believe, this island or a large part of it were subjugated and starving, then our Empire beyond the seas, armed and guarded by the British Fleet, would carry on the struggle, until, in God's good time, the New World, with all its power and might, steps forth to the rescue and liberation of the Old.

The New World. Churchill, Stephenson, and the men around them had long been convinced that ultimate salvation lay across the Atlantic, in America. But could the United States be roused from its isolationist dream to intervene before it was too late? If eloquence could not sway the Americans (it *did* sway many) perhaps events would awaken them to their mortal peril—disastrous events that now swept across Europe with stunning speed. On June 10 Mussolini's Italy declared war on Britain and France (FDR declared, "The hand that held the dagger has now plunged it into the back of its neighbor."). On June 14, while French Premier Paul Reynaud tearfully radioed, begging "clouds of planes" from America, triumphant German divisions marched into Paris. On June 21 a new French government, headed by the aged, defeatist Marshal Henri Pétain and riddled with traitors and collaborationists, surrendered unconditionally to the Nazis. Hitler, within a matter of weeks, had made himself master of an empire stretching from the Arctic Circle in Norway to the Spanish Pyrenees, from the French Atlantic coast to Warsaw. Against his huge armies and air fleets a disarmed Britain stood alone.

But not entirely alone, for she had powerful friends across the North Atlantic.

Months earlier, when he'd first returned to his old position as First Lord of the Admiralty, Churchill had opened a private and secret correspondence with Franklin D. Roosevelt. Signing himself "Naval Person"—which, when he became prime minister, he changed to "Former Naval Person"— Churchill addressed FDR as POTUS (President of the United States). The two politicians had long admired each other. They spoke not only the same language, but held the same ideals, the same perceptions of the world, and their correspondence was soon that of old and trusted friends. In his letters Churchill, from the beginning, laid bare Britain's plans, her hopes, her fears, and above all her weaknesses. He also warned of the consequences of a British defeat, which would leave an unarmed America alone to face the overwhelming power of a Nazi-organized Europe. But FDR needed no convincing on that score, nor did his closest associates, men such as Presidential Adviser Harry Hopkins; Secretary of War Henry Stimson; Secretary of the Treasury Henry Morgenthau, Jr.; Chief of Staff George C. Marshall; and many others in the American political and military establishment. Like FDR, these men understood very well that America's security depended upon continued British resistance, and that resistance depended in turn upon American aid. But their hands were tied.

For despite Hitler's victories in the west, very many— probably most Americans—still felt that the war in Europe was none of their business. And besides, America was protected against aggression by two mighty and, they believed, uncrossable oceans. Most American newspapers insisted that the United States preserve strict neutrality, and most Congressmen agreed with that view. Only by the smallest majority did Congress allocate funds to create a "two-ocean navy" in the spring of 1940, and only by an even tinier majority could it be persuaded, in the fall of that year, to pass a Draft Act to expand the Army. Like the British before them, Americans were reluctant to heed "warmongers" and so emerged from the thirties all but defenseless against the approaching storm. The American navy was too small and too antiquated for its tasks; the United States Army consisted of just 125,000 officers and men; the Army Air Corps had but a handful of fighters and bombers. And American industry, stimulated by British advance orders, was only beginning to tool up for war production. When Premier Reynaud begged for "clouds of planes," or Churchill asked for tanks, there were simply none to send.

Worse than all that, 1940 was a Presidential election year. FDR was seeking a third term in office, something no other American president had ever won or sought. And his opponent in the race, Republican Wendell Willkie, was tireless, intelligent, and loaded with charisma. True, Willkie paid lipservice to the idea of aid for Britain, but if FDR lost, then Willkie's backers and sponsors would certainly cling to isolationism. Indeed many Willkie supporters had organized themselves into something called the "America First Committee," which claimed millions of members. America Firsters listened to some impressive voices. They were told by U.S. senators that FDR was "looking for trouble" overseas in order to prolong his New Deal "dictatorship" over the nation; they were told by newspaper publishers like William Randolph Hearst and "Colonel" Robert R. McCormick that Hitler was not the monster painted by "British propagandists" and that smart people could do business with the Nazis; they were told by celebrities such as Charles A. Lindbergh that Hitler was unbeatable and Britain doomed in any case.

Churchill, an astute politician himself, well understood Roosevelt's dilemma. With American opinion confused and divided the president had to tread warily: If he acted too boldly in support of Britain he risked not only defeat in the coming election but even, many of his advisers feared, impeachment proceedings in Congress. Yet Churchill had once written, "The maneuver that brings an ally into the field is as important as that which wins a great battle." To bring this ally into the field would require the utmost intelligence, discretion, and daring—all qualities possessed in abundance by William Stephenson. After the fall of France in June 1940, Churchill dispatched Stephenson to America as his personal secret representative to FDR. The prime minister bestowed upon him then the code name that most accurately described his personality: Intrepid.

With the president Stephenson soon established a close and intimate relationship. His policy was one of absolute candor and frankness. He revealed in detail to FDR all of Britain's weaknesses as well as her strengths, though he did not at that time reveal the existence of Ultra. Many Americans were worried about what would happen to the British fleet should England be conquered. Churchill was content to let the worriers believe that the Royal Navy would retire to the New World to carry on the struggle. But to FDR Stephenson revealed that in the event of a German conquest there would probably be no more British Fleet, for the Royal Navy intended to throw its entire strength into the battle, come what may. Meanwhile, the British army had

lost almost all its equipment at Dunkirk. It had only a handful of tanks, little military transport, few field artillery pieces;
some divisions lacked even rifles. And Hitler might launch an
invasion of England at any moment: Aid for Britain could
not wait until after the November presidential election, it
was needed *now*. And, Stephenson assured the president,
any help he sent would be put to immediate and determined
use. Britain would fight an invasion with no holds barred.
She planned to use mustard gas against German beachheads
and to rouse her civilian population to unprecedented guerrilla war under the suicidal slogan "You can always take one
with you!"

Roosevelt listened and was convinced; he decided to ac-
cept the political risks. Under an old and obscure law it was
discovered that the president, as commander-in-chief, could
dispose of military supplies as he saw fit "in the best interests of the United States." Seizing upon this legal nicety,
FDR ordered U.S. armories stripped of their reserves of rifles,
machine guns, and field artillery. One million obsolete
Springfield bolt-action rifles, sixty thousand machine guns,
and nearly a thousand World War I 75-millimeter cannon
were quietly rushed to east-coast ports, secretly loaded onto
waiting British freighters, and dispatched to England. It was
a measure of Britain's desperate need that the convoys carrying these old and inefficient weapons were considered the
most important ever to cross the Atlantic.

But acting as a link between Churchill and Roosevelt was
not Stephenson's only mission in the New World. He was
also assigned the task of creating from scratch a British
propaganda, counterespionage, sabotage, and economic warfare organization that would guarantee, in case Britain went
down, the continuation of the secret war against Hitler.

Renting offices in New York's Rockefeller Center, Stephenson brought into being an "information center" known
vaguely as British Security Coordination, whose ambiguous
and inoffensive-sounding name masked, as we shall see,
sometimes murderous activities. Of course, to wage war
upon and from the neutral soil of the United States was a
complete violation of American law, but Stephenson enjoyed
the support of FDR and, by presidential directive, of J.
Edgar Hoover and the Federal Bureau of Investigation. "I'm
your most valuable secret agent," Roosevelt once told him.

Cooperation between the BSC and the FBI was essential
but tricky. Hoover did not take kindly to British flouting of
American law, of which he considered himself the guardian.
Furthermore, the formidable FBI director considered his
own well-trained agents fully capable of dealing with German spies, saboteurs, and propagandists; he resented the
British intrusion. He was also well aware that Stephenson
was urging FDR to set up an American equivalent of the
BSC, which would, Hoover foresaw, limit FBI jurisdiction.
But Stephenson quickly sized up Hoover as a man who put
the reputation of his cherished FBI ahead of everything,
including American security interests. When Stephenson
promised that the BSC would give the FBI *all* credit and
plenty of publicity for every BSC success, he won Hoover's
grudging support.

The man Stephenson hoped would head an American version of BSC was his old friend William J. Donovan. The two
had met in 1916 and had kept in close touch ever since.
Stephenson knew that Donovan shared his own perceptions
of the Nazi menace and his own eagerness to combat it. A
big, bluff, hearty man thirteen years older than Stephenson,
Donovan had plenty of experience with European politics

and intrigue; he'd traveled through Europe during the First World War as an observer and agent for the American War Relief Commission. Later he commanded the "Fighting Sixty-ninth" Regiment on the Western Front—where his exploits earned him his nickname, "Wild Bill"—and after the armistice was a State Department agent in Bolshevik Russia. Although during the twenties Donovan devoted most of his energies to his corporate-law practice, he maintained his European contacts and, on visits to France, Germany, and England, witnessed the decay of the democracies and the rise of Hitler. When Roosevelt was elected in 1933, Donovan joined the Justice Department, where he soon earned a reputation for aggressiveness yet strict impartiality as the leading New Deal "trust buster." FDR fully appreciated Donovan's abilities, and during the thirties the two men developed a close personal relationship, despite the fact that Donovan was a Republican. He made several trips to Nazi Germany as Roosevelt's personal agent in the years before 1939, and the reports he brought back to FDR paralleled those Stephenson made to Churchill. So when, in June 1940, Stephenson urged the president to send a personal agent to England who could confirm his picture of British resistance, both men had Donovan in mind.

When he arrived in London early in July 1940, Donovan posed as an American businessman looking for munitions orders, but Churchill made sure that FDR's special agent was shown every aspect, including the most secret, of Britain's war effort. Wild Bill saw Home Guard battalions armed only with pitchforks and ancient fowling pieces; he saw regular-army units training with automobiles labeled Tank; he saw the pipelines leading down to invasion beaches that would convert potential German landing areas into furnaces of oil fire; he saw the daily RAF reports of battle in the skies over England; and he saw the famous "hole in the ground," the complex of bomb shelters under Whitehall from which Churchill conducted the war. He met the redoubtable Colonel Colin Gubbins, now "training gangsters" for an organization known as Special Operations Executive (SOE), whose eventual aim was to "set Europe ablaze" through "butcher-and-bolt" raids, assassinations, sabotage, and any other means the fertile imaginations of the Baker Street Irregulars could devise. He was shown the operations of MI-5's XX (for Double-Cross) Committee, which turned captured Nazi agents into tools of British Intelligence. And he was briefed on British research, then far in advance of American, on atomic fission. When Donovan returned to Washington early in August, he reported to Roosevelt that the British definitely meant business and ought to be supported at any and all costs. Donovan's mission confirmed FDR's personal inclinations and bolstered his determination to aid Britain despite the shrill warnings of American appeasers.

One of the shrillest of these was none other than the American Ambassador in London, Joseph P. Kennedy. An early supporter of Roosevelt, Kennedy had grown more and more upset over FDR's New Deal reforms, and on the subject of aid to Britain Kennedy grew positively hysterical. Britain wasn't fighting for democracy or freedom, he claimed, only for the preservation of her empire. Besides, Britain was finished: Within a matter of weeks Hitler's legions would be marching into London; American aid to England was simply pouring water down a rat hole. And, like so many other men of wealth, Ambassador Kennedy believed that Americans could do very profitable business with Hitler, provided they didn't aggravate *der Führer* by hopelessly siding with his enemies. When Kennedy learned of Donovan's mission to London, he did everything possible to sabotage it by telling influential English friends that Donovan was simply a scandal-seeking journalist.

It may be wondered why Roosevelt put up with an Ambassador in the vital London post who was so obviously a defeatist and whose views were so diametrically opposed to the president's own. The puzzle perfectly illustrates FDR's dilemma during that election summer of 1940. Kennedy often boasted—and few disputed him—that he could sway the votes of sixteen million Catholics, especially Irish Catholics in the United States. At the very least he controlled politics in his native Massachusetts and was highly influential in New York. His defection might just cost Roosevelt the upcoming election. On balance FDR decided that the damage Kennedy did in London was less than that he might do at home. So the ambassador was kept in London until late October, when he was recalled to Washington and relieved of his duties by the president. Yet Kennedy emerged from what must have been a grim meeting with FDR to announce his support for the president in the coming election! For by that time British Intelligence had amassed a sheaf of documents on Kennedy's activities that showed them to border closely on treason. Stephenson placed these papers in Roosevelt's hands and Joe Kennedy, confronted with them, saw discretion as the better part of valor. It was said that Joseph Kennedy ruled his family with an iron hand; yet many years later one of his sons, President John F. Kennedy, would make Winston Churchill an honorary citizen of the United States for his stouthearted defense of freedom "during the dark days and darker nights when Britain stood alone."

The days began darkening during the first week of August 1940, when Hitler unleashed the full force of the *Luftwaffe* against England. It was the first step in his plan, called Operation Sea Lion, to invade and subdue the British Isles. Neither the German army nor the German navy would attempt a cross-Channel invasion until the RAF had been driven from English skies. That task, Hermann Göring assured his *Führer*, would take the *Luftwaffe* only a few weeks. The Battle of Britain had begun, and as it raged on over the next few months, no man could foretell its outcome.

But Winston Churchill took no chances. Although he remained confident of Britain's ability to survive the Nazi air onslaught and would even have welcomed a German invasion, which he expected to drown on the high seas, the prime minister hedged his bets. He did this by sending one of his scientific advisers, Sir Henry Tizard, known as "Tizard the Wizard," to Washington in mid-August with dozens of crates containing blueprints, plans, documents, working models, and thousands of scientific papers—Britain's entire research armory of secret weapons. It included everything from the latest details of British atomic research to the brand-new cavity magnetron, a device that would enable radar to be mounted on planes and ships; from the most recent British submarine detection equipment to blueprints for jet aircraft. It was an incredible collection of secrets that would help arm America in case Britain should fall. The U.S. Office of Scientific Research and Development called it "the most valuable cargo ever brought to our shores." It was more than that. It was a reciprocal act of faith on the part of one nation to another such as has rarely been equaled. If Roosevelt had confidence in Britain, Churchill's confidence in the United States was even greater. Half-American himself on his mother's side, the British prime minister never doubted the arrival of that day when "the New World in all its power and might steps forth to the rescue and liberation of the Old."

Yet that liberation might be indefinitely postponed unless the RAF defeated the *Luftwaffe* in the skies over England. But in their lonely struggle against great odds, the British fighter pilots had help of which they knew nothing. For it was during the summer of 1940 that Ultra came into its own. For months the Turing engine had been seeking to decode the *Luftwaffe*'s Enigma messages at a faster and faster rate. By July the German air force codes had been so thoroughly penetrated that Göring's orders to his air fleets were reproduced at Bletchley almost as soon as they were issued. Thus the British air commanders often knew where German fighters and bombers would strike before they left their bases in France and could concentrate RAF reserves to meet them—often but not always, for German battle orders were sometimes transmitted by telephone. On those occasions the British had to rely entirely on warnings they received from their coastal radar, another English invention that, in 1940, the Germans neither possessed nor understood. Ultra and radar between them gave the air marshals of the RAF a strategic and tactical advantage of immeasurable importance over the *Luftwaffe*.

But it was an advantage that could only be exploited through the weaponry, skill, and devotion of RAF fighter command. For the *Luftwaffe* was not seeking to avoid combat: on the contrary, its primary target was the RAF itself.

Day after day during that fearful summer of 1940, waves of hundreds of *Luftwaffe* fighters and bombers roared into English airspace, and day after day the badly outnumbered English fighters scrambled from their battered airfields to meet them. It was soon apparent that British Spitfire and Hurricane fighters were superior to the German Messerschmitts, but despite heavy *Luftwaffe* losses all through July and August, the German superiority in number began to tell. By September 6 the English were throwing in their last reserves; worse than that, the infrastructure on which the RAF depended—its southern radar stations and underground command posts, its forward airfields—had been battered into uselessness. A few more days or weeks of grinding attrition and the Germans would win. Then Hitler could begin his invasion, for which thousands of tugs and barges and dozens of divisions had been gathered in the Channel ports.

Then, on September 7, the Turing engine at Bletchley began to issue its familiar sound of thousands of knitting needles clicking together. When the machine stopped, its decoded message was rushed to London. It was Hermann Göring's order to his air fleets to stop their daylight attacks on the RAF and shift to the night bombing of English cities. Neither Churchill nor his air marshals could suppress their jubilation. By the smallest of margins the RAF had won the air war over Britain! For no matter how badly the *Luftwaffe* battered English cities in night terror raids, by abandoning its direct attack on the RAF it gave up all hope of winning air superiority over Britain. And when on September 15 the Germans attempted a massive daylight attack on London, Ultra gave warning. The RAF concentrated its fighters and on that day shot down so many enemy planes that the *Luftwaffe*'s bombers never even reached their target.

It was one of the war's great turning points. Unable to achieve victory in the skies above Britain, Hitler canceled plans for the invasion of England, a decision soon known to Churchill through Ultra. The courage and skill of a mere handful of British fighter pilots, guided by secret information, the source of which would remain a mystery for decades to come, had stopped the mighty German war machine in its tracks. As Churchill rose to pay tribute to the RAF in Parliament, he may well have been thinking also of the tireless code breakers at Bletchley when he declared, "Never in the field of human conflict was so much owed by so many to so few."

Yet, if Hitler could not defeat the RAF, he hoped to destroy English civilian morale and the British war industry through the massive, indiscriminate bombing of English cities. Beginning in September, night after night many hundreds of German bombers rained death and destruction upon London. Large parts of the city were obliterated, thousands were killed and wounded, hundreds of thousands made homeless. Against these savage attacks there was at that time little defense. Night fighters were nonexistent and antiaircraft guns thundered more for the sake of civilian morale than in any hope of shooting down attacking bombers. Ultra warnings of these raids were of little avail because the means of taking advantage of them did not exist. Nor could they always be correctly interpreted.

For example, during the second week of November, Ultra intercepts revealed that the *Luftwaffe* planned heavy raids on three targets code-named *Einheitspreis* (Unit Price), *Regenschirm* (Umbrella), and *Korn* (Corn) in an operation called Moonlight Sonata. The name of the operation suggested the next night of the full moon (November 14–15,

1940) as the target date. The intelligence analysts at Bletchley correctly guessed that Unit Price meant Wolverhampton
(Unit Price = sixpence at Woolworth's = Wolverhampton)
and Umbrella meant Birmingham (Umbrella = Neville
Chamberlain, who was famous for carrying one = Chamberlain's home town = Birmingham), but to what city did *Korn*
refer? There was an area in London known as Cornhill, and
it was assumed that the attack would again be on the English
capital.

That assumption was wrong. *Korn* meant Coventry, an
ancient provincial city famous for its cathedral. On the night
of November 14–15 that defenseless town was utterly de-
molished, with great loss of life, by a massive *Luftwaffe*
attack. The fact that Ultra had predicted the German raids
gave rise, more than thirty years later, to the baseless legend
that Churchill, forewarned of Coventry's fate, had elected to
do nothing to prevent it in order to preserve Ultra's secrecy.
This untrue myth was rooted, however, not in Ultra's ac-
complishments but rather in its limitations. Even clearly
decoded Enigma dispatches required incisive, sometimes in-
spired interpretation; Coventry was martyred not by a decision of the British government but by a failure of analysis
and, of course, by Nazi savagery.

On the other side of the Atlantic that savagery was having
a long-range effect unlooked-for by Hitler. As Americans
heard on their radios night after night the accounts of foreign correspondents such as Edward R. Murrow ("This is
London . . ."), admiration for the courage of the British
people enduring the endless Nazi hail of death combined
with sympathy for their sufferings and outrage against those
who inflicted it to effect a growing shift in American public
opinion. Though isolationists might remain in a majority,

many millions of Americans were becoming convinced that Britain's fight was really theirs. They helped that November to reelect Franklin D. Roosevelt to the presidency by a substantial majority. And their increasingly vocal support was just what FDR required to combat domestic appeasers and clear the decks for action abroad.

The War Diary

October 28, 1940/Italy invades Greece.

December 8, 1940/British army in Egypt routs Italian forces.

February 11, 1941/Congress passes Lend-Lease Act assuring American supplies to Britain.

February 15, 1941/German Field Marshal Erwin Rommel and his *Afrika Korps* arrive in Libya.

March 5, 1941/British troops land in Greece to help fight Italians.

April 6, 1941/Germany invades Yugoslavia and Greece.

April 6–April 10, 1941/Rommel's *Afrika Korps* drives British from Libya back to Egyptian border.

May 27, 1941/The Royal Navy sinks German superbattleship *Bismarck* in mid-Atlantic.

June 21, 1941/German forces invade Russia on a wide front.

July 6, 1941/Japan occupies all of French Indochina.

July 15, 1941/United States embargoes shipment of scrap iron and oil to Japan.

August 9, 1941/Roosevelt and Churchill meet and agree upon Atlantic Charter of mutual war aims.

December 7, 1941/Japanese attack Pearl Harbor.

December 8, 1941/The United States declares war on Japan.

December 11, 1941/Germany declares war on the United States.

THE *INTREPID* NETWORK   4

A department of the British Government in
New York City requires several young women,
fully competent in secretarial work . . .
Those selected can expect to serve for the
duration of the war . . .

TORONTO TELEGRAM,
HELP WANTED ADS,
JANUARY 5, 1941

The doorman of the Hotel Astor on Times Square saw it
happen like a nightmare in slow motion. It was 5:30 A.M. on
a blustery March morning in 1941; the sky was still dark,
the streets deserted except for a few pedestrians muffled
against the cold, a few cars and taxis pausing for the red
light at Seventh Avenue and Forty-eighth Street. A hotel
guest had just left the Astor a few minutes earlier. The doorman watched him bend into the wind as he walked quickly
down the avenue to Forty-third Street. There, at the corner,
the man turned left and started to cross Seventh Avenue. At
that moment the light at Forty-eighth Street turned green
and the nightmare began. As the small huddle of waiting
vehicles started forward, very slowly, it seemed to the doorman, a taxi surged into the lead. The hotel guest, halfway

across the broad and empty avenue, glanced up, saw the taxi approaching, and paused to let it pass. At the last moment, while the doorman's warning shout froze in his throat, the taxi very deliberately swerved into the hotel guest, knocked him down, and sped away. Then, from nowhere it seemed, a black sedan hurtled forward, drove over the prostrate victim, turned right into Forty-second Street, and disappeared.

By the time an ambulance arrived the hotel guest was dead. He was identified as one Julio Lopez Lido, and the police, despite the doorman's story, were inclined to list him as the victim of a simple hit-and-run accident. But the police were not the only ones interested in Mr. Lido's fate. A few days after the accident several FBI agents turned up at the Hotel Astor. They examined the hotel register—which showed Lido, though of Spanish birth, to be a resident of Shanghai—and meticulously searched Lido's room and luggage. Later the FBI advised the New York Police Department not to press their investigation too energetically. . . .

The FBI's attention was drawn to this not uncommon street accident by their analysis of certain letters written by German spies in America to an address in Portugal. These letters, intercepted by the British in Bermuda—as was all correspondence between the United States and Europe—contained, between the lines of innocuous gossip, vital convoy information written in invisible ink. And one of the letters reported that someone named "Phil" had been knocked down by a taxi in Times Square and then run over and killed by a second car. "Phil" was obviously Lido—but who was Lido? To get an answer the FBI contacted British Security Coordination in Rockefeller Center. The case already bore some of the earmarks of a BSC operation.

William Stephenson reluctantly informed the FBI that Lido was actually a captain in German Military Intelligence named Ulrich von der Osten, the head of a Nazi spy ring in the United States. Von der Osten, the BSC reported discreetly, had been "eliminated." Stephenson's reluctance to reveal this information was based on the fact that BSC had obtained it from highly secret sources within the German consulate general in New York. If these valuable anti-Nazi contacts were to remain useful they had to be protected. But based on the clues Stephenson felt he could safely supply, the FBI quickly rounded up an entire German espionage network. As for the unfortunate Lido/von der Osten, like the New York Police, the FBI did not press their investigation into his death too energetically. If the death car had been driven by a British agent, J. Edgar Hoover didn't want to know about it.

The "elimination" of Nazi spy masters in America was only one of the multitude of activities in which BSC was engaged. With the same relentless energy and imaginative intelligence that had created entire industries before the war, William Stephenson, in little less than a year, had built an intelligence empire in America such as had never been seen before. BSC's agents numbered more than 3,000 and were drawn from every quarter—Americans, Canadians, British, Latin Americans, European refugees from a host of nations and from every walk of life. There were movie stars like Greta Garbo and Leslie Howard, who acted as couriers; writers such as Noel Coward, who gathered economic intelligence in South America; famous historians; magicians; criminals of every variety; businessmen; technicians of all kinds; scientists; and even, yes, taxi drivers. Stephenson demanded of them imagination, competence, courage, and above all a deeply personal moral commitment to the fight against Nazism.

One of BSC's most important outposts in America was the British crown colony island of Bermuda. Here, in a subterranean labyrinth beneath the pink stucco Princess Hotel, some 1,200 expert cryptanalysts examined all postal and telegraphic correspondence between the New World and the Old. Airmail in those days of U.S. neutrality was carried back and forth to Europe by Pan American's huge flying boats, known as Yankee clippers. On their run from New York to Lisbon, Portugal, the clippers stopped at Bermuda for refueling. And while their passengers waited (with growing irritation at prolonged and unexplained delays), mail carried by the clipper was rushed to the Princess Hotel and there sorted and analyzed by hundreds of "trappers" expert in opening and reclosing sealed envelopes so as not to leave a trace. Two hundred thousand letters could be "trapped" while a clipper waited.

What the trappers sought were small telltale signs that a message was false—for example, German sentence structure or awkward usage in a letter written in English, a page of personal gossip that lacked self-coherence, or a business letter revealing that the writer knew little about the intricacies of the business in which he was presumably engaged. Such suspicious letters were turned over to cryptologists and chemists for analysis. One of the world's leading secret-ink experts, Dr. Stanley Collins, headed the team of chemists, who could subject some 15,000 letters to various tests during a clipper layover. A special liaison unit from Bletchley coordinated the work done in Bermuda with Ultra intercepts that might provide missing pieces to an espionage puzzle.

American cryptologists and FBI agents were also, though more discreetly, in evidence; it was to combined BSC–FBI letter analysis in Bermuda that Ulrich von der Osten fell victim, along with many another Nazi agent in the Americas.

If Bermuda performed the essentially defensive function of providing BSC with the means to penetrate Nazi activities in the Americas, a few acres of Canadian farmland outside Toronto on the shores of Lake Ontario provided BSC with its offensive power. This highly secret, heavily guarded area was known as Camp X, and its function was to invent, prepare, and execute the world's dirtiest tricks. Here forgers, safecrackers, and pickpockets rubbed elbows with eminent scholars, Hollywood producers, and industrial technicians; magicians and astrologists (Hitler believed fervently in astrology) mingled with hard-eyed young men preparing to parachute on suicidal missions into Nazi Europe.

Colonel Colin Gubbins, back in England training his army of "gangsters," depended upon Camp X for the disguises that would protect his agents when they entered German-occupied territory, and those disguises had to be no less than perfect. The *Gestapo* (*Geheim Staat Polizei*, secret state police) was a hard and perceptive enemy; they were adept at spotting clumsily forged cards of identity, could spot a British agent by such tiny revealing signs as the way his clothes were sewn, the color of a pencil he used, the ink in which his shirts were laundry-marked. All these minuscule details had to be absolutely "authentic." Even so, it was estimated that the lifespan of a British agent in Europe would not exceed sixty days.

The agents themselves included a high percentage of European refugees and volunteers drawn from America's many and diverse ethnic groups. While they underwent the severest kind of commando training at Camp X, the world's most accomplished forgers prepared German or French or Dutch identity documents for them. Not merely passports or cards of identity, but work papers, special passes, social security cards, drivers' licenses, birth certificates, even used theater ticket stubs were provided. Nor was it simply a matter of copying the endless forms and trivial documents of a host of European bureaucracies: The ink in which they were printed had to be an exact replica; the ink in which they were signed had to be precisely right; the paper on which they were printed had to be manufactured with the proper watermark, the proper rag content. And while these documents were being prepared, expert European refugee tailors sewed clothing with the proper forged labels, using cloth and techniques appropriate to what was available in, say, Bulgaria or Denmark, depending on an agent's ultimate destination and his "cover." Nothing was overlooked, from shoes to eyeglasses. A highly successful counterfeiter, high on the FBI's Wanted list, now devoted his considerable talents to forging all sorts of European currencies.

Thieves and pickpockets were stationed at all ports of entry, especially New York, where they might spot useful items—perhaps suitcases from Italy or clothing from Poland or writing materials and a typewriter of Belgian manufacture. Unlucky travelers possessing these items would find that their luggage had been "lost in transit" or their hotel rooms rifled. They were always generously compensated for their losses, and no doubt grumbled about the high crime rate in New York City.

And while agents were taught how to put a huge electric generator out of action with a handful of sand, or how to kill a man silently with a bit of piano wire, famous motion-picture producers and set decorators recreated, amid the dark forests of Camp X, exact duplicates of various European streets and buildings upon which they could practice. U.S. Customs agents and Scotland Yard detectives taught the latest and most cunning ways to smuggle. Hollywood makeup artists instructed agents in the art of personal disguise. A scientific research section turned innocent, everyday items into deadly weapons—explosive loaves of bread, cyanide-filled fountain pens, chunks of wood containing TNT, incendiary cigarettes, even animal manure made of plastic explosive. A visiting Canadian officer, inspecting these devices, complained that he didn't "see any article of everyday use that's safe to touch." One of the world's greatest magicians, Jasper Maskelyne, developed his arts of illusion to include the creation of entire phony armored divisions. It was at Camp X that inflatable rubber tanks, trucks, and guns were first devised, though it was to be in the Libyan desert that they baffled German Field Marshal Erwin Rommel.

A typical Camp X operation was the attack upon Nazi influence in Brazil. That influence, and the influx of German and Italian agents into South America, had by mid-1941 grown to alarming proportions. As a first step in stemming that Nazi tide, London requested BSC in New York to break the travel and communication links between Brazil and Europe. Those links were provided principally by LATI (*Linee Aeree Transcontinentali Italiane*), the Italian airline flying into Rio de Janeiro. William Stephenson considered the matter and found a quietly subversive solution.

On instructions from BSC in New York and confirmed by Colonel Menzies in London, MI-6's head agent in Italy, known only as "500," obtained several pieces of official correspondence written by General Aurelio Liotta, president of LATI in Rome. They were "lifted" from the general's out basket by an aged Italian cleaning lady in 500's employ and dispatched by so-called "safe-hand" courier—a "neutral" Swiss "businessman"—to London and thence to New York. Stephenson took the purloined letters to Camp X in Canada. There the letter paper was analyzed and duplicated; so were the inks and so was the ancient Italian typewriter, complete with defects, upon which they'd been typed. Expert forgers now composed a new letter from General Liotta on the general's personal engraved letterhead. This counterfeit was returned to Rome and deftly inserted in the general's outgoing mail.

Within days, Commandante Vicenzo Coppola, LATI's Regional Manager in Brazil, was puzzling over a frighteningly indiscreet letter from his boss in Rome. It read in part:

> Thank you for your letter and for the report enclosed. . . . There can be no doubt the little fat man is falling into the pocket of the Americans, and that only violent action on the part of the "green gentlemen" can save the country. I understand such action has been arranged for by our respected collaborators in Berlin. . . . The Brazilians may be, as you said, a "nation of monkeys," but they are monkeys who will dance for anyone who can pull the string! . . . Saluti fascisti. . . .

The "little fat man" referred to in the letter could be none other than Brazil's President Getulio Vargas, while the "green gentlemen" were obviously the revolutionary group that was attempting to overthrow his regime. Commandante

Coppola trembled. If this letter had fallen into Brazilian hands . . . ?

It had. A microfilm copy of the incriminating document was obtained by an agent of the Brazilian secret service who was also employed by MI-6 and shown to the "little fat man" himself. President Vargas, not unnaturally, flew into a rage, expelled the entire LATI organization from Brazil, and ordered the arrest of Commandante Coppola. The unfortunate *commandante*, having smelled a rat in the first place, fled but was caught just as he was about to cross the border into Argentina carrying a suitcase containing $1,000,000 in LATI funds. He languished in a Brazilian jail for the rest of the war, wondering how General Liotta could ever have been so stupid as to write so compromising a letter, while Liotta in Rome wondered what Coppola had done to arouse President Vargas's wrath. At a stroke BSC had cut communications between the Axis powers in Europe and South America and paved the way for Brazil's later entry into the war on the Allied side.

Perhaps the most exotic and certainly the most important of all Stephenson's spies in the New World was the beautiful young woman code-named "Cynthia." Tall, with auburn hair, large green eyes, and a willowy figure, Cynthia conquered men like Napoleon conquered nations—easily and thoroughly. Married to an older British diplomat named Arthur Pack, she was actually American, born in Minneapolis and raised all over the world since her father, a U.S. Marine Corps major, was constantly being reassigned to embassy guard details. Her husband, cool, languid, career-oriented, remained indifferent to his wife's emotional needs until inevitably she began to take lovers. It was while the Packs were stationed at the British embassy in Warsaw in

1938 that MI-6 recruited Cynthia. Why did she willingly enter the dangerous world of espionage? Partly because of the excitement it promised, but mainly because she was extremely intelligent and idealistic enough to want to fight Nazism. It was Cynthia who first revealed to MI-6 the existence of X and of his willingness to recreate an Enigma machine for British Intelligence, information she had wormed out of her lover at the time, an aide to Polish Foreign Minister Jozef Beck. Just as Knox and Turing were arriving in Warsaw to interview X, Arthur Pack and his wife were leaving, transferred to South America for a reason Pack was never told; German agents in Warsaw were growing suspicious of Cynthia. Then, after several months at the British embassy in Chile, Pack was told that while he would remain in Santiago, his wife was needed elsewhere. Whatever he may have felt, the complaisant British diplomat made no objection.

Elsewhere turned out to be Washington, DC, where, late in 1940, under her maiden name of Elisabeth Thorpe, Cynthia was established by BSC in a modest two-story house on O Street in the fashionable Georgetown section. She was, she told friends and acquaintances, separated from her husband and working now as a free-lance journalist for various English magazines and newspapers.

Soon after her arrival in Washington, Cynthia called upon an old friend from prewar days in Paris, Admiral Alberto Lais, now a naval aide at the Italian embassy. While discussing old times with his charming visitor, Admiral Lais confessed himself disappointed with the turn his career had taken. He'd always hoped for a fighting command but here he was, condemned to idle away the war in a neutral capital, middle-aged, saddled with a large family, without hope of further advancement. But Cynthia—how refreshing to see her again! She reminded him of more carefree days.

The admiral began to visit Cynthia's house on O Street—secretly, of course, to avoid malicious gossip. He was not at all disturbed by Cynthia's open avowal of the British cause: He'd always opposed Italy's alliance with Nazi Germany and he feared for his country's future in this idiotic war. These clandestine meetings elevated the admiral's depressed spirits; what did he have to do all day except decode boring cable-grams? Yes, he was custodian of a complete set of Italian naval ciphers at the embassy, but his duties were no more than those of a clerk. Cynthia sympathized, charmed, se-duced. Yes, the war between Britain and Italy *was* unneces-sary, ridiculous, harmful; the Germans were *everybody's* enemies. The sooner Italy quit the war the more she would be spared. And the admiral could help. Cynthia had some very good friends among the officers of U.S. Naval Intelli-gence, she said, and they'd told her of U.S.–British plans to liberate Italy from German domination. Now, if only Ad-miral Lais would allow her to "borrow" those Italian naval codes for microfilming, he'd be well rewarded personally and make a real contribution to his country's future. Unbe-lievably the admiral agreed, and within a month of her ar-rival in Washington, Cynthia was able to transmit this abso-lutely vital information into the hands of the admiralty in London. It was British possession of these codes that led the Royal Navy to fall upon an Italian fleet off Cape Matapan, Greece, on March 28, 1941, and inflict upon it so crushing a defeat that never again during World War II would Italy challenge English naval dominance of the Mediterranean

Sea. As for Admiral Lais, his usefulness now at an end, the U.S. Government pronounced him *persona non grata* and he was recalled to his homeland.

The effect of Cynthia's activities was direct, immediate, and catastrophic, but not all BSC's undercover plots had such clear-cut results. Sometimes it was a question of tipping a balance, of providing a final straw. Such was the case with Bill Donovan's journey to the Balkans.

The origins of this strange mission went back to the fall of 1940, when Ultra had revealed Hitler's decision to move his armies to the east in preparation for an all-out attack on the Soviet Union. Called Operation Barbarossa, the Nazi plan envisaged the complete destruction of Russia within six months. The assault would begin in May and be over well before the torrential autumn rains made Russian roads impassable or the grim Russian winter froze German tanks in their tracks. For the next several months Ultra messages passed through British hands, giving the details of the tremendous German deployment eastward. Churchill, through Stephenson, kept Roosevelt well informed about all this.

Since his triumphant reelection in November 1940, FDR had felt much more secure politically, and therefore more willing to take risks in the struggle against Hitler. He'd persuaded a recalcitrant Congress to repeal the last of the Neutrality Acts, which hamstrung American aid to Britain, and during the winter of 1940–1941 was carefully shepherding through the Senate and House the Lend-Lease Act, which would transform the United States into "the arsenal of democracy." Nonetheless, isolationist sentiment was still extremely strong in America and Roosevelt had to tread warily, offering every step of the way explanations that would disarm his critics. For example, when he declared the entire

North and South Atlantic Oceans west of longitude 26° to be a "Hemispheric Defense Zone," it was understood publicly that the U.S. Navy would peacefully patrol those waters to "keep the fighting away from American shores." It was not revealed that the U.S. Navy would also cooperate with the Royal Navy in escorting convoys or that American warships would seek, identify, trail, and report to the admiralty on German U-boats and surface raiders. And sometimes FDR had to act in complete secrecy from his countrymen, as when, in January 1941, the American and British chiefs of staff conferred in Washington to settle on worldwide plans for the destruction of Hitler.

Those chiefs of staff, examining Ultra evidence of Nazi plans against Russia, agreed that Operation Barbarossa might very well succeed unless it could somehow be delayed. If it could be delayed for a month or six weeks, then the German offensive would run into the terrible Russian winter and perhaps fail. It was no use warning the Soviets of the impending German onslaught. Both Churchill and Roosevelt had repeatedly placed irrefutable evidence of Hitler's plans before Stalin. But the Russian dictator, a captive of his own prejudices, fears, and paranoia, dismissed all warnings as a British-American plot to embroil him in war with his German ally. If Russia was to be helped it would have to be *in spite* of Stalin. Could Hitler be diverted for a few weeks? If so, where?

The Balkans, of course—that treacherous quicksand of national hatreds, shifting political alliances, and unstable governments. The Balkans would be on the flank of a German attack on Russia and the German general staff would demand absolute security in the region. This Hitler was in the process of assuring through treaties with the Fascist-inclined governments of Hungary, Romania, and Bulgaria and through pressure upon the weak government of Yugoslavia, which was then a kingdom, ruled by Prince Paul, regent for the boy-king Peter. There was a further complication in the Balkans, this one provided by Hitler's pompous and woolly-minded ally, Mussolini. Having seized the tiny country of Albania in 1939, *Il Duce*, in December 1940, had launched his Fascist armies against neighboring Greece. But the hardy Greeks proved more than a match for the Italians and, within a few weeks, had driven them far back into Albania itself. The British, who had recently destroyed an entire Italian army in North Africa, offered to help, but the Greeks, fearing German intervention in that case, politely declined. It is questionable whether Hitler would have intervened in Greece merely to salvage his ally's reputation, but the possibility that a British Expeditionary Force *might* appear in the area was troublesome. It will be seen, then, that the Balkan tinderbox was smoking: could Hitler be precipitated into igniting a real conflagration there?

FDR, Stephenson, and Churchill considered the matter, and late in January 1941 Bill Donovan was dispatched on a presidential "fact-finding" mission to the Near East. Publicly it was announced that Donovan would inspect British forces and installations in Egypt, Palestine, and Libya in order to determine how much and what kind of American Lend-Lease aid they required. He might also visit a few Balkan capitals to assess the current political situation there. That was the first, most obvious "cover story." But Nazi intelligence forces were not to be deceived by so simple a tale. They knew there had to be more to Donovan's travels than that.

They found the proof they needed while Donovan was

visiting Sofia. There the American presidential representative tried to persuade Bulgaria's King Boris to reexamine his country's pro-German policies. In this he failed: Bulgaria was firmly committed to Hitler. Worse than that, while Donovan was discussing matters with the king his hotel room, luggage, and clothing were rifled through by German agents. They found in the lining of a sport jacket, a series of coded notes. Microfilms of these papers were rushed to Berlin.

Having failed to persuade King Boris, Donovan now journeyed to Belgrade. There he urged the Yugoslav regent, Prince Paul, to resist Nazi demands. But the Nazi agents who dogged Donovan's footsteps noted that he did not limit his visits to official government circles: he also had lengthy "secret" talks with General Richard Simović, Chief of the Yugoslav Air Force, and other known anti-Nazi military officers. Then, as suddenly as he'd appeared in the Balkans, Donovan vanished, to reemerge a few weeks later in Washington, DC. What had he been doing in the meantime?

When German Intelligence decoded the microfilms of Donovan's notes they found the outlines of British-American plans to ignite war in the Balkans and lists of prominent officials in various Balkan governments who were prepared to resist the Nazis. Hitler's suspicions, already aroused by Donovan's tour of Balkan capitals, were deepened. His attention was distracted from the vast preparations for Operation Barbarossa. The Anglo-Saxons were obviously plotting trouble on his right flank. He'd give them all the trouble they could handle.

Of course, Donovan's notes were phony: They'd been carefully prepared by BSC experts at Camp X, encoded, and sewn into one of his jackets where, it was hoped, Nazi operatives would have little difficulty in finding them. They were a hoax intended for German eyes—and the hoax succeeded. But it would be too much to claim that Donovan's mission alone pushed Hitler into war in the Balkans. *Der Führer* always intended to secure his southern flank before marching into Russia—by diplomatic means if possible, military if necessary. Then, too, there was the question of Mussolini's disgraceful showing against the Greeks, which damaged Axis prestige generally and offered the British an excuse to intervene. Like many another BSC operation, the Donovan mission was intended to ignite Hitler's paranoid suspicions, adding to real events in the real world just that imaginary coloration that might provoke *der Führer* to rash, ill-judged action.

That action, when it came in April 1941, was sudden, massive, and savage. Having already extorted permission from Hungary and Bulgaria for the free passage of German troops through their territories in order to attack Greece, Hitler demanded that Yugoslavia also sign a treaty of alliance with Germany. Prince Regent Paul and his government speedily caved in before *der Führer*'s threats, but Air Force General Simović and several other high-ranking officers staged a palace revolution in Belgrade, deposed Prince Paul, and proclaimed the boy-king Peter monarch. Then they politely turned down the German demands. Hitler flew into one of his rug-eating rages. At his command the city of Belgrade was obliterated by continuous *Luftwaffe* attacks while German *Panzer* divisions plunged into both Greece and Yugoslavia. The British rushed a small expeditionary force to Greece, but it arrived only to share in the general defeat. Within a few weeks Hitler had made himself master of the Balkans.

A few weeks—that was the price. To be precise, the deployment and redeployment of German forces involved caused a six-week delay in the timetable of Operation Barbarossa. So that instead of attacking Russia in May, the Germans struck in June. Their final assaults on Moscow and Leningrad came in late November and were quickly bogged down in mud and snow. Speaking to their Allied captors after the war, surviving members of the German general staff agreed that the six-week delay had been fatal to their chances of a quick victory over the Soviet Union. BSC deserves at least part of the credit.

British-American cooperation produced a brilliant success in the Donovan mission. However, the failure of that cooperation produced tragic errors from time to time. The most glaring of these was probably the case of the double-agent known as Tricycle. Tricycle was the British code name for a middle-aged Yugoslav aristocrat named Dusko Popov. Popov had been blackmailed into joining the German intelligence service in 1939. After war broke out he was given a small radio transmitter and smuggled into England by way of neutral Lisbon. Once safely beyond the claws of the *Gestapo*, Popov turned himself in to the British. He was placed under the control of the XX (Double-Cross) Committee, which, as we have seen, specialized in the manipulation of captured German agents. For the next several months, under British supervision, Popov used his wireless set to feed German Intelligence a steady mix of true but useless information.

Pleased with Popov's performance in England, the Germans ordered him to transfer his operations to the United States in June 1941. Passing through Lisbon on his way to New York, Popov was handed a long list of questions about

American defenses in which German Intelligence had a particular interest. Of course Popov showed his questionnaires to William Stephenson as soon as he arrived in New York. But now problems arose.

Popov, on American soil, had to be turned over to the FBI for "handling"—such was BSC's agreement with J. Edgar Hoover. But Hoover was a severe and unforgiving Puritan regarding the personal morals of anyone who worked for him, while Popov was a flamboyantly decadent European playboy. Wherever he traveled, Tricycle was accompanied by a gaggle of mistresses, crates of champagne, sagas of lurid gossip: his very code name had been bestowed upon him by the British in recognition of his propensity for bedding two women at once. There was a brief meeting in Washington between Hoover and Popov, which ended badly. So badly that BSC was "urged" to get Popov out of the country as quickly as possible. As for the Yugoslav's questionnaires about American defense establishments, little attention was paid to them; they were filed and forgotten.

Which was a shame, for Popov's questionnaires included a large section of precise, detailed, and exceedingly specific inquiries regarding American air and sea defenses of the great Pacific naval base at Pearl Harbor, Hawaii. Anybody pondering these carefully prepared questions might well have concluded that someone must be planning a direct attack on the place. . . .

Someone was, but not Popov's German masters. For despite the fact that American Lend-Lease war supplies were pouring into Britain; despite the fact that the U.S. Navy was waging an undeclared war against German U-boats; despite such provocations as the Donovan mission; by the spring of 1941 it was becoming apparent that if war came to America it would come in the Pacific, not the Atlantic. For this there were several reasons.

First of all, although the United States was one of his eventual targets, Hitler did not want war just yet—not while his armies were totally immersed in Operation Barbarossa. For after their six-week excursion into the Balkans, on June 22, 1941, the German dive-bombers and *Panzer* divisions had burst into the Soviet Union along a two-thousand-mile front. Heedless of Allied warnings, Stalin went into a month's hiding in the Kremlin while the mighty German forces ground up entire Russian armies and destroyed most of the Red air force on its airfields. Nazi motorized and armored columns plunged hundreds of miles into the vast expanses of Russia, brushing aside all opposition. The world held its breath. Could Russia survive this onslaught? Churchill announced full British support for the Soviet Union, remarking to an aide, "If Hitler invaded hell, I would at least make a favorable reference to the Devil in Parliament," while Roosevelt ordered Lend-Lease supplies extended to the USSR. Until the outcome of the titanic struggle being waged between the Nazi and Communist dictatorships could be definitely known, Hitler sought to avoid complications elsewhere; he even refused Field Marshal Erwin Rommel the very modest reinforcements with which the "Desert Fox" might well have swept the British from the entire Near East at the time. Besides, *der Führer* counted upon Japan to keep America preoccupied; it cost him nothing to urge the Japanese to "act boldly" in the Far East.

The Japanese hardly needed urging. Still bogged down in their endless war against China, Japanese militarists and imperialists saw the German victories in Europe as presenting a heaven-sent chance for the fulfillment of their goals in the

Orient. The great western empires—the French, the Dutch, the British—had been defeated and bled dry by Hitler. Now was the time for Japan to pick up their pieces in the Far East.

In preparation for this, Japan had joined Germany and Italy in September 1940 in a so-called "Tripartite Pact," which stated that should any of the three powers be attacked by a nation "not then at war," the others would come to her aid. The only significant nations "not then at war" were Russia and the United States. When Russia did become embroiled, in June 1941, she had not "attacked" Germany and Italy, and so Japan was not bound to make war upon the Soviet Union. In fact, during the summer of 1941, Japan concluded a nonaggression treaty with Russia that, as the cynical Stalin observed, "freed [Japan] to turn south." Thus, there was no question against whom the Tripartite Pact was aimed: It was aimed against the United States. The question facing Japanese leaders was simply whether or not the Americans would sit idly by while Japan conquered all of the eastern Pacific. Probably not, they decided, but America was still unready for war, and if Japan acted swiftly, she might carve out an oceanic empire so strong that even a rearmed United States might hesitate to seriously attack it. Such was the theory, at any rate, put forward in Tokyo.

The theory was put to an early test when, as the first step in their expansionist program, the Japanese occupied the French colony of Indochina. The vigor of the American response was both shocking and definitive: It was nothing less than a full embargo on trade with Japan, including trade in scrap iron and, above all, oil. This was serious. The Japanese had only enough oil stockpiled for ten months' peacetime use, six months' wartime. The only place she might get more oil was the Dutch East Indies, but since the Dutch complied to the American embargo, that could only be accomplished by conquest. Yet, an attack on the Dutch East Indies meant almost certain war with the United States. Furthermore, the decision for peace or war would have to be made speedily, while Japan still possessed enough oil to conquer more oil. Negotiations were opened between Japan and the United States in Washington upon which the Japanese set a secret deadline. If no progress was made by late November 1941, a military solution would be sought.

Most of this was well known to Roosevelt and the American military chiefs from their interception of Japanese diplomatic and naval messages through Magic, the American equivalent of the Turing engine. And there now loomed before FDR and his close advisers one of the great potential disasters of World War II: What if Japan made war upon the United States but Hitler did not? The American people would then surely demand that all United States war supplies and military energies be devoted exclusively to the Pacific, leaving Britain and Russia alone to face the still-conquering Nazi war machine in Europe. The United States might even win a war against Japan, only to find Hitler absolute master of the European continent, including the British Isles. At the secret American-British chiefs of staff meeting held in Washington early in 1941, it had been decided that Hitler was by far the most dangerous enemy, and no matter how much damage Japan did in the Orient, American-British strategy must concentrate on defeating Germany first. But unless *der Führer* declared war on the United States, American isolationist opinion would by no means permit this strategy to be applied.

Here was another case in which a fabricated straw might

tip the balance of Hitler's unbalanced mind. While war clouds gathered over the Pacific, BSC, with FDR's full blessing and J. Edgar Hoover's cooperation, expertly forged at Camp X, in Canada, a series of documents entitled the Victory Program and purporting to be the verbatim decisions of those secret British-American staff conferences. The Victory Program outlined plans for deeper and deeper American involvement in the struggle against Hitler, no matter what Japan did or did not do in the Far East. American provocations were to grow and grow until *der Führer* would have no choice but to declare war. If he did not, the Americans would fall upon him anyway in 1942 or 1943, depending how things went in Russia. Like all good fakes, this forged Victory Program contained just enough truth to be plausible. But how to get it into Hitler's hands without arousing Nazi suspicions?

A copy of the Victory Program was "stolen" from top-secret U.S. Army files by an Army captain who took it to Senator Burton K. Wheeler, a leading America Firster, a bitter foe of Roosevelt, and a great advocate of appeasing the Nazis. As was anticipated, the senator's patriotism was far weaker than his hatred of FDR. He did not hesitate to release these supposedly top-secret documents both to the rabidly isolationist *Chicago Tribune*, which published them, and directly to the German embassy in Washington. They were, of course, immediately dispatched to Berlin and received there as absolutely authentic.

Who can tell what weight this forgery had with *der Führer*? When, on December 7, 1941, Japanese bombs rained down upon Pearl Harbor, Hitler, as surprised by the attack as anyone else, told his cronies that Germany would now have to declare war on the United States in order to stand by their Japanese ally. Besides, it was now clear that Russia was crushed and "would never rise again," so that German forces could soon turn back to the west and the conquest of Britain. "But that is not the main reason," he added. "The chief reason is that the United States is already shooting at our ships. They have been a forceful factor in this war and through their actions have already created a situation of war." So Hitler had more solid motives for declaring war on the United States than simple paranoia. Yet, when *der Führer* addressed a cheering Reichstag on December 11, 1941, he used the words: "Our enemies must understand that it is *we* who will *always* strike the first blow!" Which sounds very much like a veiled response to the Victory Program.

When Churchill had first dispatched William Stephenson to the New World as Intrepid, one of the great tasks assigned him was to help Roosevelt "guide" America into the war against Hitler and to help prepare Americans for the inevitable battles ahead. As much as any one man could, Stephenson had brilliantly fulfilled this assignment. Now, at last, Britain and America were full and open partners in the war against Hitler and Churchill, having already declared war on Japan, "went to bed and slept the sleep of the saved and thankful."

The War Diary

January 1, 1942/German offensive stalls before Moscow.

January 7, 1942/Rommel repulses British offensive in Libya.

January 15, 1942/Russians open counteroffensive against Germans.

January–April 1942/Japanese conquer Southeast Asia, threaten Australia and India.

THE ADMIRAL AND THE HANGMAN 5

Wouldn't you find all this quite comical
if it weren't so desperately serious?

ADMIRAL WILHELM CANARIS

They were nearly invisible against the dark clouds of a midnight sky—six black-clothed figures dangling from six black
parachutes only fitfully outlined against a half-moon as they
fell swiftly into wooded hills near the Czechoslovak town of
Lidice. As each man landed he quickly slipped from his
harness and began furling his chute; when all six were down
the parachutes were dragged to a shallow pit and buried.
Then and only then did the men who had prepared the pit
emerge from hiding—stealthy figures who led the para-
chutists away into the night. The Anthropoids had arrived,
right in the middle of Hitler's Europe in mid-December
1941, on a deadly mission that would, as its authors were
well aware, eventually cost the lives of many thousands of
innocent men, women, and children; a mission so dangerous

that those who volunteered for it were, from that moment, considered dead.

Operation Anthropoid had been carefully designed by the chiefs of British Intelligence, Menzies and Gubbins, to accomplish a very immediate and urgent task, but the origins of this desperate venture may be traced a long way back in time. . . .

It began perhaps as far back as the days of the First World War, when in 1916 a twenty-nine-year-old German naval officer, Captain Wilhelm Canaris, formerly of the raiding cruiser *Dresden* (scuttled under British guns off the coast of Chile) was sent as a naval intelligence officer to neutral Spain. There, despite recurring bouts of malaria, Canaris proved so adept at finding out the routes of Allied merchant ships that German U-boats in the Mediterranean began reaping a terrible harvest. British Intelligence took note and an officer from MI-6, a Captain Stewart Menzies, was sent to Spain to either capture or kill Canaris. But despite some incredibly narrow escapes, Canaris eluded Menzies, made his way back to Germany, and became a U-boat commander himself, eventually sinking some eighteen Allied ships in the Mediterranean. It was the first and only time the two future chiefs of their countries' intelligence services met in the field, but it was the beginning of a long and strange entanglement.

Like Menzies, Canaris stayed on in intelligence work after the war—with even more secrecy, since Germany was not supposed to have an intelligence service—and in 1934 was appointed by Hitler to be chief of the *Abwehr*, the central, all-embracing intelligence section of the German general staff. It is not certain why Hitler chose him. Canaris was an aristocrat who could not help regarding *der Führer* as a slightly comical guttersnipe; he favored restoring the Kaiser to the throne in Germany, and he was not even a member of the Nazi party. Perhaps it was simply an early example of Hitler's intuition at work; if so, it was dangerously misleading.

Not that Canaris proved inexpert in his new duties. On the contrary, by 1938 he had built up a powerful network of agents throughout Europe, deeply entrenched everywhere, but especially in neutral Sweden and Spain. What made the appointment of the distinguished-looking (he was short, slim, spectacled, rigorously polite, and possessed of a full mane of white hair of which he was vainly proud) admiral dangerous to Hitler's ambitions was the fact that Canaris loathed Nazism and dedicated his very considerable abilities to its destruction. It was in his office that the *schwarze Kapelle* came into being, under his cover that emissaries had been sent to England before the war warning of Hitler's plans and aggressions. We have seen that these warnings were ignored for a variety of reasons and that the *schwarze Kapelle* plots to overthrow Hitler inevitably foundered on prewar Allied appeasement policies. Once war was declared, Canaris's role became even more dangerous, for he had to provide enough intelligence to satisfy Hitler and the German high command while at the same time seeking, through calculated intelligence leaks, to undermine their success—all the while dealing with a British intelligence service that might or might not take him seriously.

A typical Canaris operation was his sabotaging of Hitler's plan to seize Gibraltar, Britain's mighty fortress guarding the western entrance to the Mediterranean. This plan, Operation Felix, was devised as a subsidiary blow to accompany the main invasion of England, Operation Sea Lion. In mid-July 1940, while the RAF and the *Luftwaffe* struggled in the skies over Britain, Hitler dispatched a reconnaissance team to Spain to report on the possibilities of Operation Felix. Canaris insisted on heading the team himself.

His report, submitted three weeks later, was a masterpiece of discouragement. First of all, there could be no question of a surprise attack on Gibraltar: There was only one road that led across the peninsula connecting the rock to the Spanish mainland and that was under constant observation. The steeply sloping sides of Gibraltar and the lack of landing places made an airborne or parachute attack impossible. The British were exceedingly well entrenched and all but immune to bombing. The recently reinforced garrison might be reduced by artillery bombardment, but this would require the deployment of not less than a dozen regiments of the heaviest guns—regiments that the German high command, as Canaris well knew, could not spare from the buildup for Operation Sea Lion itself.

And finally, no German assault upon Gibraltar could even be undertaken without the fullest cooperation and assistance of the Spanish government. This assistance Hitler had every right to expect: After all, it had been German and Italian support that had given Spanish dictator General Francisco Franco victory in the bitterly contested civil war. Yet, somehow agreement between the two dictators was always elusive.

For this there were two excellent reasons. The first was that with his nation still prostrate from the civil war, Franco had no desire to enter another conflict. The second was that Canaris strengthened Franco's resistance to *der Führer*'s demands. For example, when Spanish Foreign Minister Ramón Serrano Suñer, Franco's brother-in-law, made a trip to Rome, he was approached by one of Canaris's top agents,

Dr. Josef Mueller, who whispered, "The admiral asks you to tell Franco to hold Spain out of this game at all costs. It may seem to you now that our position is the stronger. It is in reality desperate, and we have little hope of winning this war. Franco may be assured that Hitler will not use force to enter Spain." In Madrid Canaris personally told Franco that an excellent delaying tactic would be to ask Hitler for a dozen fifteen-inch guns, since Germany had no such guns and it would take years to manufacture them.

When on October 23, 1940, Hitler met personally with Franco at Hendaye in the French Pyrenees, the Spanish dictator was confident enough of his position to keep *der Führer* waiting two hours and then subject him to so many evasive remarks that Hitler later declared he "would rather have four teeth out than go through that again." Operation Felix was abandoned, a casualty of Canaris's expert intrigue. Hitler, of course, never realized that he'd been frustrated by his own intelligence chief. In fact, his confidence in Canaris and the *Abwehr* remained unbounded.

Unfortunately, however, Canaris's treasonable intrigues had already aroused the suspicions of one of the most influential and dangerous of Hitler's followers, Reinhard Tristan Eugen Heydrich, a long-time personal friend of Canaris and, since 1932, chief of the *Sicherheitsdienst* (SD), the intelligence service of Heinrich Himmler's dreaded SS and of the Nazi party itself. Just as the SS was a private army of fanatics within the German armed forces, so the SD was a private intelligence service within the Nazi state, outside Canaris's control and a rival of the *Abwehr*.

Heydrich was young—he'd been born in 1904—extremely intelligent, utterly ruthless, and cut from the same cloth of moral monstrosity as Hitler himself. But unlike *der*

Führer, Heydrich was a man of great accomplishment. He spoke half a dozen foreign languages fluently and was a first-class fighter pilot, an outstanding sportsman, and a highly polished musician: It was his excellent playing of the violin that first attracted Canaris's attention when, in 1923, both men were stationed aboard the German cruiser *Berlin*. Canaris was a captain then and Heydrich a mere ensign happy to ingratiate himself with a higher-ranking officer. Signals Officer Heydrich, who was also an expert cryptographer, might have achieved high rank in the German navy, but in 1931 he became involved in a complicated sexual scandal and was court-martialed and dismissed from the *Kriegsmarine* "for impropriety."

Now an outcast, Heydrich naturally gravitated into the ranks of the party of outcasts, the Nazis. He was introduced to Heinrich Himmler, who was then forming his SS. Impressed with this new recruit, Himmler assigned Heydrich the task of creating a separate SS and Nazi party intelligence and security organization. This he did so efficiently that his efforts soon attracted the attention of Hitler himself. Heydrich, *der Führer* decided, was the absolute epitome of what a Nazi ought to be—was, in fact, so pure and efficient a "superman" that he became Hitler's first choice as his own successor. Virulently anti-Semitic, Heydrich had organized mobs throughout Germany in November 1938 to launch murderous attacks on their Jewish neighbors in what became known as the "Night of Broken Glass."

As Heydrich's private intelligence empire, the *Sicherheitsdienst*, began to grow, its agents infiltrating every sector of German life, Admiral Canaris took steps to protect himself and the *Abwehr*. He compiled a dossier on Heydrich that revealed that this pure superman had homosexual proclivities and—most horrible sin of all in Nazi Germany—Jewish ancestors. This information was deposited with a Swiss bank under instructions that it should be immediately forwarded to *The New York Times* if anything "untoward" happened to Canaris or his family. Having thus taken out this "insurance policy," the admiral informed Heydrich of what he'd done, and remarkably the two men remained friends—as friendship went in Nazi Germany.

With the onset of war Heydrich's star rose even higher in the Nazi firmament. It was he who was given the task, by Himmler, of "eliminating" the leadership classes in conquered Poland, a task Heydrich performed so well that an estimated two million Polish intellectuals, businessmen, schoolteachers, politicians, trade unionists, and other "troublemakers" were murdered within six months of the fall of Warsaw. Perhaps because of his success in Poland, Heydrich was later assigned by Himmler to design and create the system of genocide that would eventually result in the death of six million Jews and millions of other "subhumans" in the terrible extermination camps of Eastern Europe. Until his death, in fact, Heydrich was in direct charge of the "final solution to the Jewish problem," a task later taken over by Adolf Eichmann. In the spring of 1941 Heydrich was made "protector" of Bohemia and Moravia, the former provinces of Czechoslovakia, with instructions to follow the same program he'd undertaken in Poland. This assignment, however, proved to be Heydrich's death warrant.

For others besides the Nazi hierarchy had been watching Heydrich's career with great interest: British Intelligence Chiefs Menzies and Gubbins. They agreed that Heydrich was a formidable enemy; more than that, he was a living symbol of everything Hitler's Germany stood for and was

Hitler's probable successor. He was also the scourge of the conquered nations of Europe and a mass murderer of great efficiency. Yet, all of this was not decisive to his unseen judges in London. What was decisive was the fact that he was becoming exceedingly dangerous to Admiral Canaris and the *Abwehr*. Should Heydrich finally outmaneuver the suave little admiral and take over *Abwehr* operations, MI-6 would lose its most valuable ally inside Hitler's Europe. The judges conferred in London and sentence was passed: Heydrich must die.

Colonel Gubbins chose two men from the Czech army-in-exile, Jan Kubis and Josef Gabcik, and sent them to Camp X in Canada. There they were intensively trained for their mission. They practiced amid Hollywood sets organized by movie producer Alexander Korda to reproduce various sections of the city of Prague. There was even an exact replica of Heydrich's green Mercedes-Benz limousine. But even as they practiced with submachine guns and grenades, disaster struck the Czech underground.

Heydrich, always anxious to find a lever to pry Canaris loose from his intelligence empire, had tortured from a captured Czech underground agent news of the existence of Franta, the code name of an unidentified German traitor who could only be one of the senior executives of *Abwehr* headquarters in Dresden. Franta, it seemed, had been passing information to the British since 1936, mainly through the Czech underground leaders, the so-called Three Kings who operated in Prague. Heydrich did not, of course, know exactly what information Franta had passed along; if he had he would have been horrified. For Franta had forwarded in the greatest detail all the German high command's plans and operational orders as well as detailed information on *Ab-*

wehr and SD organizations throughout Europe. He had warned of German moves against Austria, Czechoslovakia, Poland, Norway, the Netherlands, Belgium, France, and the Balkans, and his information always checked out with Ultra decodings: It was absolutely reliable. But who was Franta, what were his motives, and, of great importance, what were the sources of his information? He simply knew too much for one man. He knew so much, in fact, that he could only have been serving as a mouthpiece for Canaris himself.

As soon as he took up his new duties in Prague, Heydrich set out to crush the Czech underground and, if possible, expose and capture Franta. Acting on information supplied by a Czech traitor, the *Gestapo* captured the first of the Three Kings, a Czech Lieutenant Colonel named Balaban, on April 22, 1941. A few weeks later, on May 13, *Gestapo* agents raided an apartment in the old quarter of Prague. Inside were the second and third of the Three Kings, Czech Colonel Masin and Captain Vaclac Moravek. They were transmitting information to London by wireless when the Germans burst in. Colonel Masin drew a revolver and blasted his way out of the apartment to the stairs, killing three *Gestapo* men in his rush. But he caught his foot in the bannister, broke his leg, and was captured alive. Meanwhile, under cover of the gunfire, Captain Moravek tied the aerial of his wireless set to the leg of a sofa, tossed the loose end out a window, and slid down it to the street four floors below. By the time he landed he'd sheared off one of his fingers on the sharp wire, but he escaped, made his way to another wireless post, and warned London of what had happened. Then he went into hiding. Colonels Masin and Balaban were executed by the *Gestapo* after much torture, but they died with their lips sealed. They couldn't have given

Heydrich the information he wanted anyway. Only Moravek knew the man called Franta.

Moravek's warning was decisive in London: the Anthropoids were dispatched immediately to kill Heydrich. But by the time they arrived on that cold December night in the hills outside Lidice, Heydrich had already learned the true identity of Franta. He was, it turned out, an old and trusted Nazi party member named Paul Thummel, who was chief of *Abwehr* operations in the Balkans with headquarters in Prague. London ordered the Anthropoids to postpone the killing of Heydrich in order to rescue Thummel if possible.

Thummel himself was arrested on February 22, 1942, and interrogated by the *Gestapo*—gently, since his rank was too high to permit rough treatment. He told his captors that he'd been trying to penetrate the Czech underground through his contacts with Moravek and would have succeeded but for the blundering of the *Gestapo* men who arrested him. As for Franta, he knew nothing of any such person or name. Canaris, on learning of his agent's arrest in Prague, rushed to forestall Heydrich by placing the entire case before Heinrich Himmler. Himmler swallowed Thummel's story and directed that he be released, which was done on March 2, 1942. Round one to Canaris. But the game was not over.

On the evening of March 22, the *Gestapo* learned that Moravek was to meet one of his subagents, Stanislau Rehak, code-named "the Dandy," at 7:00 P.M. in a little park next to Prague's Convent of Loretta. The *Gestapo* staked out the park and, when the Dandy appeared at 7:10 P.M., they closed in. Rehak was immediately captured, but Moravek, who'd been sitting on a bench, leaped into some nearby bushes and, a gun in each hand, shot it out with his pursuers. He lost the battle and within a few minutes the last of the

Three Kings was dead. Worse than that, under torture, Rehak revealed enough to tie Thummel firmly to Moravek. Thummel was rearrested immediately and held on suspicion of high treason.

At last Heydrich had the evidence he needed to break Canaris and the *Abwehr*. But Canaris was not to be easily subdued. He came to Prague in person on May 21, 1942, to meet Heydrich and discuss the entire situation. Yes, the admiral had to admit that the *Abwehr* had evidently been penetrated at certain levels by British Intelligence. And yes, it might be better if the SD took over counterintelligence operations. As for a merging of the *Abwehr* and the SD, that was a matter that would require prolonged thought and study. As soon as their meeting ended, Canaris gave verbal orders to his lieutenants that the agreements he'd reached with Heydrich were to be ignored. But how long could the admiral keep Heydrich at bay? London ordered the Anthropoids to strike at once.

The first thing the assassins had to do was find an exact place and time to attack their victim, and in this they had luck. It seemed that an antique clock in Heydrich's office wasn't working properly and a Czech repairman, Josef Novotny, was called in to set it right. Novotny placed the clock on Heydrich's desk to begin dismantling it when he noticed a piece of paper with Heydrich's hour-by-hour itinerary for March 27 typed on it. He crumpled the paper into a ball and tossed it into the wastebasket. Shortly afterward, having fixed the clock, Novotny left. Minutes later one of the cleaning ladies, Marie Rasnerova, entered Heydrich's office and emptied the wastebasket into her sack, and within a few hours the itinerary was in the hands of the Anthropoids.

At 9:30 A.M. on the morning of March 27, Kubis and

Gabcik, along with two members of the Czech underground, armed with machine guns and grenades, waited in the bushes alongside the road leading to Hradcany Castle, Heydrich's headquarters. At this spot the road made a hairpin bend down to a bridge: any car passing down the road would have to come to an almost complete stop to negotiate the curve. A fifth member of the Czech underground was positioned in a hedge at the beginning of the curve. He was to signal with a mirror when Heydrich's limousine actually approached.

At 10:31 A.M. light flashed from the hedge. Gabcik stepped into the road, his submachine gun at the ready, aiming at the bend. Heydrich's big green Mercedes came into view, slowing for the curve. Gabcik pulled the trigger—and nothing happened: His gun was jammed. Heydrich and his chauffeur both stood up in the Mercedes and shot down Gabcik with drawn pistols just at the moment when Kubis threw a grenade right into the car. There was a terrific explosion, Heydrich collapsed, and amid the ensuing commotion Kubis and the three Czech underground men escaped.

Heydrich was rushed to a hospital and there, on June 4, 1942, he died—not of his wounds but of gangrene. The lord of the Nazi terror system had been killed in broad daylight, with as many of the circumstances of a public execution as the Anthropoids could devise. The German vengeance was terrible. Over ten thousand people were arrested in Prague, of whom at least 1,500 were killed. The village of Lidice, which the Germans wrongly suspected of harboring the assassins, was wiped from the face of the earth. All its male inhabitants from the age of sixteen up were herded together in the village square and machine-gunned; its women and children were hustled onto trucks and carried away, some to slave labor in Germany, some to hideous medical experiments, some to extermination camps. Few were ever heard of again. Then the town itself was utterly destroyed by fire and dynamite.

Meanwhile the Anthropoids had gone into hiding in the crypts of the Karel Borromaeus Greek Orthodox Church in the old town of Prague. They secreted themselves in narrow niches in the stone walls that had originally been built to hold the corpses of monks. There they waited until the Czech underground could devise a plan for their escape. The idea was a good one: A mass funeral would be staged for some of the victims of the *Gestapo*'s vengeance in Prague and the Anthropoids would be taken from the church in several of the coffins. Then they would be spirited away into the Moravian mountains, where they could be picked up and returned to London. A good plan, but it was betrayed by a man named Karel Curda, who was greedy for the $600,000 reward the *Gestapo* had placed on the Anthropoids' heads.

When, on June 19, 1942, the mass funeral began, the Karel Borromaeus Church was suddenly surrounded by SS shock troops and *Gestapo* men. They forced the church sexton to take them inside, but as the SS troops made their way down the aisles they were met with a burst of gunfire from the choir loft, where Kubis was hiding. Kubis was killed with a hand grenade. The SS men then tried to get into the church basement and were again greeted with a hail of bullets. An SS officer called in the Prague fire department to flood the basement. It was the end. The Czech underground agents hiding in the basement, down to their last cartridges, shot each other one by one, the last man shooting himself. The Anthropoids' mission was over.

Reinhard Heydrich's body, dressed in the black and silver uniform of the SS, lay in state for two days in the courtyard of Hradcany Castle. Then it was shipped on a black-draped train to Berlin. Hitler himself placed a corsage of orchids on the bier as he praised Heydrich, "the man with the iron heart." Himmler made a long, rambling speech to his assembled SS officers, during which he pointed out that their intelligence operations still "could not compare with those of the British Secret Service," as Heydrich's corpse proved. One of the high Nazi officials who watched these proceedings quietly was Admiral Wilhelm Canaris. At the graveside he even managed to produce a few tears.

The War Diary

May 8, 1942/Japanese naval forces defeated by Americans in the Coral Sea.

May 20, 1942/German offensive drives toward Stalingrad and the Caucasus.

June 4, 1942/American navy defeats Japanese at battle of Midway.

June 20, 1942/Rommel forces British back to El Alamein, sixty miles from the Suez Canal.

August 30, 1942/Germans reach Stalingrad.

October 28, 1942/British defeat Rommel at El Alamein.

November 8, 1942/British and American armies invade French North Africa.

December 31, 1942/German forces at Stalingrad surrender to Red Army.

May 12, 1943/German forces in Tunisia surrender to Allied armies.

"... AN ORIGINAL AND SINISTER TOUCH" 6

Practically all the ruses and stratagems
of war are variations or developments of a
few simple tricks that have been practiced
by man on man since man was hunted by man.

GENERAL SIR ARCHIBALD WAVELL

When it came to "ruses and stratagems," General (soon to be Field Marshal) Wavell certainly knew what he was talking about; with few other resources available he'd used "a few simple tricks" to utterly destroy the entire Italian empire in Africa. It had seemed an almost comically impossible feat at the time. Here was the vainglorious Italian Marshal Rodolfo Graziani invading Egypt in September 1940, driving toward the Nile and Britain's vital Suez Canal lifeline to the Orient. Should the Italians break through in Egypt, then trade, raw materials, military supplies, and reinforcements passing back and forth between India, Malaya, Australia, and Britain would have to make the long trip around the southern tip of Africa, for the Mediterranean route would be closed. Furthermore, beyond Egypt itself there were few

British forces to oppose an Italian drive into the Near East, into Palestine, Syria, Lebanon, and beyond, perhaps to the gates of India. Turkey, with an Italian army on her southeastern border, might well join the Axis powers, oil from Iran would be cut off, and the blow to British prestige might disrupt the Empire and cost Churchill his leadership.

Graziani's forces were huge: some 200,000 men equipped with hundreds of tanks, thousands of pieces of artillery, trucks, and all the mechanized panoply of mobile war. To oppose this mighty host General Wavell could muster but 35,000 poorly equipped, almost tankless men and his own wits. He also had the help of Brigadier Dudley Wrangel Clarke, a staff officer recently arrived in Egypt from London. A highly successful lawyer in peacetime, Clarke was also a student of the tactics of such imaginative rebels as the Boers, the Irish Republican Army, and the Confederates during the American Civil War.

The problem was how to persuade Graziani to stop his advance in its tracks and keep the Italians immobile long enough for reinforcements to reach Wavell from England. Clarke and Wavell pondered the matter and soon a stream of requests was reaching London, requests not for tanks and guns, which simply were not available, but for thousands of specially designed, inflatable balloons! These were hastily manufactured and airlifted to the Western Desert.

Soon the British defense lines facing Graziani's forces blossomed with hundreds of cruiser tanks that could be packed into cracker boxes when deflated, field artillery pieces that emerged from small ration boxes, and heavy trucks that came two to an ammunition case. Then Clarke sent engineers to lay dummy roads and tracks south of Sidi Barrâni, where Graziani's army lay, and large crowds of

Arabs with camels dragging two-by-fours behind them to raise huge clouds of dust. When observed from the air by Italian reconnaissance planes, all this looked like a mighty armored force moving down on Graziani's right flank. The Italian marshal ordered his forces to halt, dig in, and hold fortified positions where they were.

The trick worked. Graziani lay apprehensively immobile while Wavell concentrated his small forces for an attack. The British struck on December 9, 1940, sending small, mobile columns far to the west of Graziani's mighty host to cut their communications and supply lines. The Italians panicked, and by February 7, 1941, Wavell's men had advanced 650 miles into Italian Libya and taken 130,000 prisoners, 400 tanks, and 1,300 guns—all at the cost of 500 British dead. At the same time, using the same deceptive tactics, a tiny British army in the Horn of Africa, at a cost of 135 killed, captured 50,000 prisoners of the army of the Duke of Aosta, conquering Italian East Africa and liberating Ethiopia in the process. Mussolini's African empire had not only been destroyed, but the Italian martial spirit was fatally and irretrievably punctured. As *Il Duce* and his marshals reflected on these disasters back in Rome they were both frightened and puzzled. Something mysterious seemed to have taken place.

Just "a few simple tricks." Years before, when writing of his experiences during the First World War, Winston Churchill had reflected, "There is required for the composition of a great commander not only massive common sense and reasoning power, not only imagination, but also an element of legerdemain, an original and sinister touch, which leaves the enemy puzzled as well as beaten." Now, with the success of "ruses and stratagems" so triumphantly confirmed in

North Africa, Churchill organized, early in 1941, a committee of the heads of Britain's intelligence and special-operations forces to be known as the London Controlling Section (LCS). Menzies, Gubbins, the heads of MI-5, MI-6, SOE—the entire numbers-and-alphabet group that ran the secret war—were members. Their overriding task was to devise deceptions to fool the enemy in the field, to make him think an attack was coming when it wasn't, to make him believe huge armies existed where they did not, to make him prepare for blows in one place that would be delivered in another.

It was well that Churchill brought the LCS into being when he did in April 1941, because just a few weeks earlier, in mid-February, on the heels of the Italian defeat in North Africa, Hitler had dispatched three German divisions, two of them armored, to retrieve the situation in Libya. They were commanded by General Erwin Johannes Eugen Rommel, a brilliant soldier whose own "original and sinister touch" would earn him the title the Desert Fox, make his *Afrika Korps* legendary, and force the British to the cliff edge of disaster in North Africa.

Rommel was a small, silent, businesslike man who had joined the Kaiser's army as a cadet in 1910, distinguished himself during World War I, stayed with the peacetime army between the wars, and distinguished himself again, in command of a *Panzer* division, during the conquest of France in 1940. He was short, sharp, shrewd, utterly and completely dedicated to the science of war and possessed of that rare "sixth sense" regarding strategy and tactics that distinguishes the brilliant from the merely competent commander. Although he refused to become a member of the Nazi Party, he admired Hitler and considered that *der Führer's* ideas about armored warfare came close to military genius. As we shall see, he was to change his opinions radically. Hitler, on the other hand, liked Rommel precisely because he was an outsider, not a member of that *Junker* class that made up the German general staff and had looked down upon Corporal Hitler with aristocratic contempt.

From the moment Rommel and his *Afrika Korps* appeared in North Africa, the desert campaign changed dramatically. Beginning his offensive in March 1941 against a still poorly equipped British army, now reduced by the need for reinforcements to Greece, Rommel swept forward until by June 1 he stood victorious at the gates of Egypt, waiting only for Hitler's order to march on to the conquest of Cairo, Alexandria, and the Suez Canal. But by now *der Führer's* thoughts and hopes were centered on his Russian campaign, and the order did not come.

Taking advantage of this respite from disaster, the British reinforced their desert army and in November 1941 launched a counteroffensive against the *Afrika Korps*. Rommel's forces withdrew before the British onslaught, farther and farther back into the trackless Libyan desert. The English commanders congratulated themselves on their "victory" and drove their armored brigades relentlessly in pursuit—and into the trap that Rommel had long since prepared for them. For the *Afrika Korps* withdrawal was not a rout but rather a carefully preplanned retreat cleverly designed to lure the British hundreds of miles away from their supply bases into a prefortified area where, amid minefields and the roar of powerful German 88-millimeter artillery, their armored divisions were ground to bits. By the end of December 1941 the British Eighth Army was a wreck. Allowing his enemy no respite, Rommel launched a counteroffensive in January 1942 that carried his forces once again to the Egyptian border and then, in the spring of that year, he made a swift lunge that, by the end of June, brought the *Afrika Korps* to the little desert hamlet of El Alamein, just sixty miles from Cairo and the Suez Canal. British government officials in Cairo began burning their secret documents; the British eastern Mediterranean fleet was withdrawn into the Red Sea; Mussolini ordered fancy new uniforms and a white horse upon which he expected to enter Cairo in triumph. Visiting Roosevelt in Washington, DC, Churchill confessed himself "the unhappiest Englishman in North America since Cornwallis." Erwin Rommel, the Desert Fox—a field marshal now—had inflicted upon British arms one of the worst defeats in history.

Late in June 1942 the British wireless intelligence service began hearing strange whispers on their radio sets. These were quickly identified as coming from a German wireless intelligence unit located just behind the German lines at El Alamein. The precise location of this unit was determined through radio direction-finding equipment and, on July 10, an Australian battalion was sent forward to penetrate the German lines and if possible capture the German equipment intact. The Australians were completely successful: An Italian division guarding the German intelligence unit was asleep, and their haul in documents, radio equipment, and prisoners was huge.

Now, to their dismay, the British learned some of the reasons for Rommel's "baffling" success. First of all, they learned that the Germans had penetrated the supposedly secure American "Black Code" through which American military attachés throughout the world were transmitting their daily reports to Washington. The U.S. attaché in Cairo, Colonel Frank Fellers, was no exception. Every day he duti-

fully reported to Washington such matters as British dispositions, reinforcements, equipment, morale, and plans. By
simply plucking the colonel's reports out of the ether and
then decoding them, Rommel enjoyed a perfectly clear and
precisely detailed picture of his enemy's forces and intentions. For this windfall the German commander was in-
debted to an Italian secret agent working in the American
embassy in Cairo who had picked the lock of the embassy
safe, removed the Black Code, photographed it, and then
returned it.

Of course, the Americans immediately replaced the Black
Code with another in August 1942. But at British suggestion
they continued transmitting in the Black Code such "secret"
information as the English wanted Rommel to hear.

Even more disturbing lessons were deduced from the capture of the German wireless intelligence unit—namely, that
the Germans were "reading" entirely too much British military radio traffic directly. Simply by listening to brief
snatches of radio conversation and orders between tank
commanders, for example, or between command posts or
artillery units, the German experts were able to deduce British plans by the volume of talk and its location. New orders
went out to tighten wireless security throughout the Eighth
Army.

Finally, among the captured German papers, the British
found references to a mysterious *Kondor Mission* located in
Cairo itself. . . .

The story was exceedingly romantic, the threat, in those
dark days of 1942, exceedingly desperate. The master of
Kondor was a young man (just twenty-eight at the time)
named Johann Eppler, who had been born of German parents in Alexandria and whose mother had married a well-to-

do Egyptian lawyer after his father's death. Thus Eppler was an Egyptian citizen and a British subject; furthermore, he'd made the holy pilgrimage to Mecca and was therefore a Muslim. He retained his German allegiance when war broke out and was recruited into Admiral Canaris's *Abwehr*. He arrived in Tripoli in April 1942 after training in Germany. With him he brought two American Hallicrafter radio transceivers, £50,000 in British money, an assistant named Peter Monkaster—a young German engineer who had lived for years in East Africa—and a copy of Daphne du Maurier's novel *Rebecca*. This book was to serve as the basis of the code in which the two agents would transmit their reports, an old and well-known cryptographic trick by which messages would be based on the prearranged use of certain pages of the novel on certain days. Though simple, the system was impenetrable so long as no one knew what book was being used.

Eppler and Monkaster, disguised as civilians, with plenty of forged identity papers and driving a captured British command car, left Tripoli for Cairo on May 11, 1942. They made a very wide detour of the British lines to the south and, after a two-thousand-mile journey, arrived at Assyut, an Egyptian town some three hundred miles south of Cairo. There, after convincing a British patrol that Eppler was an Anglo-Egyptian merchant and Monkaster an American oil-rig mechanic, the two spies caught the train for Cairo.

Had it not been for Egyptian nationalism and the fanatic hatred many Egyptians had developed for British imperialism, the *Kondor Mission* would have been fruitless. But in the climate of crisis produced by Rommel's advance, and in the ever-boiling stew of anti-British intrigues that permeated the Egyptian capital, Eppler was soon able to find the necessary help. His first recruit was Miss Hekmeth Fahmy, a famous Egyptian belly-dancer, a member of the violently nationalistic Moslem Brotherhood and already a spy for the so-called Free Officers' Movement of the Egyptian army. Miss Fahmy's main source of information was a "Major Smith" of British headquarters in Cairo—her lover, whose briefcase she regularly inspected.

Eppler and Monkaster rented a houseboat on the Nile and began transmitting Major Smith's information in the *Rebecca* code every midnight to German listening posts in Libya and Greece. And not only did Miss Fahmy supply them with much highly interesting military information, she also arranged their meeting with Sheikh Hassan-el-Banna, the slightly mad "prophet" who led the Moslem Brotherhood, and with two young Egyptian army officers, Gamal Abdel Nasser and Anwar el-Sadat, who led the Free Officers' Movement. With these fiery nationalists Eppler and Monkaster hoped to raise an Egyptian jihad (holy war) against the British to coincide with Rommel's final drive on Cairo. Sadat was especially eager; the future Egyptian president insisted that "now is the time to strike. We can turn the [Nile] Delta into a blood bath. . . ."

Perhaps overconfident, Eppler now made two serious errors. First, trying to gather the latest military gossip, he dressed as a British officer and bought drinks at both the Turf Club and the Metropolitan Hotel, paying for them with British currency. But British money was not legal tender in Egypt: it had to be exchanged for Egyptian currency through the British paymaster's office. And when the paymaster took a hard look at the pound notes presented by the two bartenders, he recognized them as German forgeries.

Eppler's second error was in picking up a bar girl named

Yvette at the Metropolitan. After buying her quantities of champagne, Eppler took her back for the night to his houseboat, paid her in British five-pound notes, and asked her to come and see him anytime. She agreed. But Yvette was an agent of the Jewish Agency, which worked with British Intelligence. She immediately reported to MI-6 that she thought Eppler might be a German spy because he spoke with a Saarland accent, had entirely too much money, and was "very nervous." Her superiors at MI-6 told her to continue meeting Eppler and arranged to place the houseboat under continuous surveillance.

A few days later Yvette once again called on Eppler. But when she arrived at the houseboat it was to find both Eppler and Monkaster sound asleep in their quarters. Quietly looking through the boat's main cabin she discovered an open copy of *Rebecca* and several notebook pages full of letters and numbers. Well aware that these were the ingredients of a code, Yvette copied down many of the entries and then silently left.

Meanwhile, several prisoners from the raid on the German wireless intelligence unit arrived in Cairo. One of them, among his personal belongings, carried a copy of *Rebecca*. But what would a German radio operator be doing with such a book, especially as it was in English? Yvette had the answer.

Early on the evening of August 10, 1942, the British security forces seized Eppler's houseboat. As they clambered abroad, Monkaster dived into the cabin, opened the boat's bilges to scuttle her, and, through a trapdoor, tossed both the Hallicrafter radio and the copy of *Rebecca* into the mud of the Nile. On deck Eppler held off the British boarding party by rolling up socks into tight balls and throwing them at the enemy. The English soldiers thought they were hand grenades and held back just long enough for Monkaster to complete his work. Finally captured, both German spies refused to talk under the most severe interrogation. But Miss Fahmy, who'd been arrested at the same time, was willing to talk freely, and from her MI-6 learned everything. Major Smith, Anwar el-Sadat, and many accomplices were arrested, but not Nasser. More important, the Hallicrafter radio and Eppler's copy of *Rebecca* were retrieved from the Nile. Although the radio was now unusable, its dials were still set at the frequency the spies had used to communicate with German listening posts. And between Yvette's notes and their own cryptographic expertise, the British were able to recreate the *Rebecca* code. MI-6 was now able to impersonate Eppler and resume broadcasting to Rommel, this time information that would lead the Desert Fox to disaster.

For Rommel was now, at the end of August 1942, ready to resume his triumphant march to Cairo. His plans, revealed by Ultra intercepts, were made known to the Eighth Army commander, Sir Bernard Law Montgomery, and, using the *Kondor* codes, Montgomery radioed back exactly what he wanted Rommel to hear. So when the *Afrika Korps* finally mounted its attack in what would be known as the Battle of Alam Halfa, its tanks ran into deep sand where they thought to discover hard ground, its vehicles ran into amassed British artillery, and its infantry into waiting British armored divisions. Rommel's army was badly beaten at small cost to the British; the threat to Cairo and the Suez Canal was removed; and, most vital of all the fruits of this defensive victory, the initiative once again passed into Allied hands. Rommel, who knew he had been tricked, could only write despondently in his war diary, "The British command had been aware of our intentions. . . ." The Desert Fox went on sick leave to Germany.

Even before the British victory at Alam Halfa, the Allied joint chiefs of staff were preparing the first of those gigantic operations that were designed to "tighten the ring," as Churchill put it, around Nazi Germany and then squeeze it until the Third Reich cracked. This was the invasion of French North Africa known as Operation Torch. Both the genesis and the matrix of the operation were political.

Ever since the German invasion of Russia, Stalin had been insisting that the Allies immediately establish a second front in Western Europe—at whatever cost. The fact that the cost could be total defeat (the Germans had constructed formidable defenses known as the Atlantic Wall all along the invasion coasts) and that the British and Americans lacked both the manpower and the specialized shipping needed for such an invasion did not weigh with the grim Soviet dictator. Russia was fighting for its very life and bearing the brunt of the German attack; what did the Allies propose to do about it? Both Churchill and Roosevelt worried that the Russians might be overwhelmed or that Stalin, as he had once before, might strike a bargain with the Germans that would remove Russia from the war. American military commanders—especially U.S. Chief of Staff General George C. Marshall—thought that some sort of descent on the French coast might be possible in 1942, but the British were convinced that this was impossible. The price that Churchill was willing to pay to convince his eager Allies that they were mistaken will be examined in the next chapter; by late summer 1942 he had won the argument. But if not in France, the Allies had to fight somewhere; that was politically essential.

French North Africa seemed the likeliest target for several

reasons. First of all, its conquest would open the Mediterranean to Allied shipping, thereby shortening by weeks the supply routes to the Near and Middle East; secondly, it would plant a large Allied army in Rommel's rear; thirdly, it would offer a springboard to the invasion of Italy and Southern Europe—what Churchill liked to call "the soft underbelly" of the Nazi empire; finally, it might bring the French back into the war against Hitler. And with luck this invasion might not prove too costly because, although the Vichy French forces in North Africa were large, it was felt that they would not fight effectively against their former allies of two world wars.

But what of the Germans? Nazi airpower in the Mediterranean, based in Sicily and southern Italy, was powerful; Nazi U-boats were plentiful; German and Italian forces could be poured into Tunisia and Libya across the narrow sea far more quickly than American and British troops could be transported from England and the United States, and Rommel's *Afrika Korps*, though beaten at Alam Halfa, was still a powerful and threatening army. While the Allied invasion fleets would be powerful, they would not be overwhelmingly so, for at this stage of the war the Allies still lacked the specialized landing craft, the airpower, and the fleets that they were later able to muster. So surprise would be a vital factor in their plans, and French cooperation essential.

To gain that cooperation it was decided to mount the invasion as an American rather than a British expedition, although British troops, ships, and planes would largely predominate. The United States still maintained diplomatic relations with the French Vichy government and the Americans were not perceived by Marshal Pétain and his defeatist supporters as a threat to the French empire overseas as were the

British. American agents were able to move freely both within Vichy territory and in French North Africa and had already approached various French politicians and military commanders to enlist their cooperation. To give the invasion its "all-American" coloring, overall command was entrusted to a previously obscure American officer, General Dwight David Eisenhower; American troops were earmarked for the initial landings; and Churchill even offered to put British troops into American uniforms.

As for the element of surprise, that was a difficult matter. The plan called for an American invasion force to land on the Atlantic coast of French Morocco simultaneously with British and American landings along the Mediterranean coast of Algeria. Since the troops bound for Morocco would sail directly from the United States, it might be possible to conceal their movement or, at the very least, their destination, but the forces bound for Algeria would have to pass through the narrow Straits of Gibraltar under open observation by German agents posted in Spain. Furthermore, very large air forces would have to be gathered at Gibraltar, not to mention vast fleets of fighting ships. It would obviously be impossible to disguise these huge preparations.

If not disguise, then misdirection. British and American agents all over the world began to carefully "leak" the news that the Allies intended to descend upon the French colonial port city of Dakar on the west coast of Africa. Radio traffic between England and Allied agents near Dakar was increased dramatically, and Allied preparations for this nonexistent invasion were broadcast in codes that MI-6 and the LCS knew the Germans had penetrated. When the Germans took the bait and concentrated dozens of U-boats in the South Atlantic near Dakar, an Allied convoy of merchant ships, returning empty from the Middle East, was purposely guided into these wolfpacks and sacrificed to maintain German delusions.

For the most part these political preparations and deception plans worked. The Germans were convinced that the huge Allied buildup at Gibraltar was destined for Dakar, and while their U-boats were sinking merchant ships off that distant city, Allied military convoys descended on their targets far to the north on November 8, 1942. But in both Morocco and Algeria, much to American surprise and mortification, Vichy French forces put up an initially bitter resistance that only ended a few days later when Vichy-French Admiral Jean Louis Darlan, a notoriously pro-German officer who happened to be present in Algiers when the Allies attacked and was captured by American troops, ordered a cease-fire.

The German reaction was swift and dramatic. While British and American troops raced east toward Tunisia, the Germans mounted a massive airlift of troops and supplies to that French colony. Though its cost was heavy, the Germans won the race and when, by mid-December, Allied troops reached the Tunisian border, their farther progress was halted by some 200,000 well-equipped and entrenched German veteran fighting men. And, disgusted by French "treachery," Hitler ordered his forces in Europe to occupy Vichy France, thereby extinguishing the last spark of French "independence." But although the German forces in Tunisia, with their much shorter supply line across the Mediterranean, held up the Allied advance from the west, disaster was approaching them from the east in the shape of the victorious British Eighth Army, fresh from a decisive victory over the *Afrika Korps* in the battle of El Alamein.

El Alamein was one of the turning-point battles of World War II. "Before it," Churchill declared, "we never had a victory; after it we never had a defeat." And this first British triumph on the long road to Berlin owed as much to field deception as to the courage of the troops involved and the tenacity of their commanders.

The deception was, once again, in the hands of Brigadier Dudley Clarke, the man who had so successfully fooled Marshal Graziani in 1940. But the problem was different now. It wasn't necessary to create a dummy army to terrify the enemy; it was necessary to disguise a very large real army from enemy eyes.

Ever since he'd stopped the *Afrika Korps* at Alam Halfa in August, British General Montgomery had slowly and patiently built up both the supplies and the morale of his Eighth Army. By October he enjoyed a comfortable superiority over Rommel's forces, but the problems he faced were many. The *Afrika Korps*, though mauled at Alam Halfa, was still a strong force, and its strength was multiplied by defensive minefields, entrenched tanks, well-prepared artillery positions, and, worst of all, geography. For the area in which the battle would have to be fought was severely circumscribed. The El Alamein position was bordered by the Mediterranean to the north and, some sixty miles away, a completely impassable area known as the Quattara Depression to the south. The front was narrow and there was little room for maneuver, and any massing of British forces would easily be spotted by German reconnaissance planes. Yet a heavy concentration of British tanks, artillery, and infantry would be needed to break through the German lines.

First of all, it was necessary to hide the gasoline that would be required by hundreds of tanks and thousands of trucks during the offensive. Clarke's men, working at night, stored two thousand tons of gasoline in barrels in a series of slit-trenches that had been dug months before and with which the Germans were perfectly familiar. From the air the shadows of these trenches effectively disguised the presence of the thousands of barrels of fuel they now contained. As for ammunition and other stores, some four thousand tons of these were brought forward and covered with netting so that, from the air, they looked like a concentration of ten-ton trucks and soldiers' bivouacs. One thousand pieces of artillery were disguised beneath other nets to look like three-ton trucks. As for the real trucks involved, these were brought forward into the attack area quite openly so that the Germans, observing their presence and noting that nothing further came of it, would relax their vigilance. There remained the problem of disguising the presence of more than 750 tanks and self-propelled guns. These were too distinctive to disguise, so they were openly massed in three groups well behind the front near a series of tracks that led south. Observing this concentration of armor, the Germans decided that any British attack would be against the southern flank of their front. To foster this misconception, when the battle finally did begin, on October 23, these tanks moved south during the late afternoon, but at night doubled back toward the north.

The rest was history. Under a barrage from one thousand guns, British infantry punched a hole in the German lines just where they were least expected. After a few days of hard fighting powerful British armored forces raced through this hole. So little did Rommel expect this attack that he was on another visit to Germany when it took place. He hurried back to his *Afrika Korps*, only to find it in complete rout.

The victorious British chased the shattered Germans across thousands of miles of North Africa, back all the way to Tunisia. And in May 1942 the Eighth Army joined British and American forces from the west to complete the conquest of all North Africa. The fighting for the continent had cost Germany and Italy some 600,000 men, 8,000 planes, 2,500 tanks, and all hope of victory in the west. Rommel, having been withdrawn from Africa to command German forces in Western Europe, visited Hitler at *der Führer*'s headquarters in Rastenburg on March 10, 1943, when the end in Tunisia was already in sight.

"Do you really think we can have the complete victory we aim at?" Rommel demanded.

"No!" Hitler replied.

"Do you realize the consequences of defeat?"

"Yes," Hitler admitted.

There was little more to say.

The War Diary

May–December 1943/The RAF and U.S. Eighth Air Force bombard German cities.

July 10, 1943/Allied forces invade Sicily.

July 25, 1943/Mussolini arrested; Fascist government ends in Italy.

August 17, 1943/Allies complete their conquest of Sicily.

August 19, 1943/British attack Dieppe and are repulsed.

August 25, 1943/Russian summer offensive has driven Germans back in Ukraine and White Russia. Siege of Leningrad is broken.

September 5, 1943/Allies land in southern Italy.

September 8, 1943/Italy surrenders to Allies.

SACRIFICES   7

We must remember that there is
a moral force in wars that in the long
run is stronger than any machine.

GEN. WILLIAM J. ("WILD BILL") DONOVAN

The dawn sky over the ancient Spanish coastal city of
Huelva on April 30, 1943, was fiery red, promising another
scorching day. Most of the town's fishing fleet had already
returned to port after a long night's work. The small craft,
hardly larger than a ship's lifeboat, owned by Juan Ferrer
was the last at sea. The boat's antique diesel engine was
reluctant to start. But by 6:00 A.M., with the sun now well
up in the eastern sky, Ferrer's motor finally coughed to life
and the weary fisherman headed home. A few minutes later,
just a mile from shore, Ferrer saw an object floating in the
water. He veered over to it and discovered a life-jacketed body,
face down to the gentle swells. Ferrer hauled the body into
his boat and sped to port. Perhaps there would be some sort
of reward: The corpse was dressed in a British officer's uni-

form and to its left wrist was chained an important-looking briefcase. As soon as his boat was docked, Juan rushed over to the Spanish naval headquarters in the port to report his grisly find. There was no reward.

But there was intense activity as the corpse was removed to a local morgue. The Spanish naval authorities telephoned the British vice-consul at Huelva to inform him that the body of a Captain (acting Major) William Martin of the Royal Marines, serial number 09560, had been recovered from the sea. The vice-consul, in turn, telephoned for instructions to Captain J. H. Hillgarth, the British naval attaché at the embassy in Madrid. Hillgarth asked the vice-consul to make very certain that the briefcase attached to the corpse was retrieved unopened and intact. But when the vice-consul asked the Spanish authorities for the briefcase he was told that it had been impounded "for judicial purposes."

Actually, as soon as the body had been placed in Spanish custody, the local officials had informed Admiral Canaris's secret agent in Huelva of the fact. And while a Spanish doctor examined the corpse and certified that it was that of a British officer who had died by drowning after an air crash, the German agent busily photographed all the documents contained in the briefcase. It was only two weeks later, after repeated requests from Hillgarth in Madrid, that the briefcase was finally returned to British authorities, apparently unopened.

Meanwhile, Major Martin was buried at Huelva with full military honors. His fiancée sent a wreath to the funeral and the British vice-consul sent Major Martin's family some photographs of the Spanish naval party firing a salute at the graveside. Later a plain white marble tombstone was placed over the grave, which read:

William Martin
Born 29th March, 1907
Beloved son of John Glyndwyr Martin and
the late Antonia Martin of Cardiff, Wales
Dulce et decorum est pro patria mori

R.I.P.

Even as Major Martin's coffin was lowered into Spanish soil, German intelligence experts in Berlin were evaluating the photocopies of the documents the major had been carrying. They were of great importance because Major Martin had been a staff officer at Combined Operations headquarters in London, and they conclusively proved that after the Anglo-American victory in Tunisia, the next Allied targets in the Mediterranean would be the island of Sardinia in the west and Greece in the East. A casual observer might have assumed that the Allies would attack the big Italian island of Sicily after they had won in North Africa, but the very obviousness of this step made it suspect. Besides, by attacking in Greece, the Allies could hope to drive north into the Balkans and endanger the southern flank of the German armies on the Russian front. As a strategic objective this made much more sense than any campaign among the forbidding mountains of Sicily. Were Major Martin's documents authentic? Without question: Personal effects, letters, even theater ticket stubs, proved beyond doubt that this was no Allied "plant."

Hitler pondered the matter. He had long felt threatened on his Balkan flank. The conquered countries of that area, Yugoslavia, Greece, and Albania were garrisoned primarily by Italian troops, unreliable in *der Führer*'s estimation. De-

spite the demands of the Russian front, Hitler detached several German divisions from the fighting there and, with other
divisions brought from France, hastily reinforced the Balkans. He also dispatched Field Marshal Erwin Rommel to
Athens to command the new front. When the Allies landed
in Greece they would get a very hot reception.

But, of course, the Allies did not land in Greece or Sardinia. Instead, on July 9, 1943, American and British armies
under the command of Generals George S. Patton and
Bernard Montgomery descended on the obvious target, Sicily. There they met little opposition and within a month had
conquered the island and were poised for an invasion of
Italy itself. Hitler and the German intelligence services had
been hoodwinked again.

They'd been tricked by an operation carried out by the
LCS and the XX (Double-Cross) Committee in London
and code-named, with grisly accuracy, Mincemeat. No effort
had been spared to make this ruse plausible. Since "Major
Martin"—a false name—was presumably to have been the
victim of an air crash at sea, it was necessary that a corpse
be found of a man who had died of pneumonia, so that it
would have water in its lungs. Such a corpse was obtained
from the London morgue; its true identity was never revealed,
and permission was obtained from the parents of the dead
man to use the body for "special medical purposes."

The corpse was packed in a cylinder of dry ice and taken
to XX Committee headquarters on Regent Street, London.
There his identity was fabricated and he was dressed in a
carefully pretorn and presoaked uniform. A complete personality and "background" was created for Major Martin,
mainly by the use of fabricated letters from his sweetheart, a
Double-Cross Committee secretary; from his bank, Lloyds

of London—showing that he had an overdraft—with personal bills, including one from a well-known London jeweler for an engagement ring; and with letters from his parents. Along with this material such items as theater ticket stubs and receipted bills, all bearing the proper dates, were placed in the major's briefcase. And, of greater importance, military documents and personal letters from Allied commanders in London to Allied generals at Mediterranean headquarters in Algiers were included. These were made just obscure enough to give German intelligence officers some difficulty in piecing together the jigsaw information that convinced them of Allied intentions. When every detail was perfect, Major Martin made his last trip—abroad HMS submarine *Seraph*, which surfaced off Huelva and, just before dawn on April 30, slipped the corpse into the sea not far from the lights of a Spanish fishing fleet.

The corpse of "Major Martin" and the feelings of his family and friends were a real if not too painful sacrifice to victory. But British Intelligence and the planners of British strategy in London, including Churchill himself, were prepared to make much greater, more violent, and less excusable sacrifices to win the war. Undoubtedly the largest and most catastrophic of these was the assault on the French Channel port of Dieppe on the night of August 19–20, 1942—Operation Jubilee.

Jubilee's origins were various. It had been originally conceived during the winter of 1941–42 as simply a very large-scale commando raid on the French coast, the purpose being to keep the Germans nervous about their Atlantic Wall defenses, to undermine the morale of German troops stationed on the Channel, and to capture certain advanced German radar and radio installations, which were to be carried off to

Britain for study by English scientists. It was hoped that the raid might induce Hitler not to send further reinforcements from the west to Russia and also, the RAF hoped, to lure the *Luftwaffe* into costly combat over the Channel skies.

But while planners in London worked out the details of Jubilee, the Anglo-American joint chiefs of staff, at meetings in Washington, were thrashing out the grand strategy of the war. The Americans, fearful of a Russian collapse, wanted to establish a second front in Europe in 1942, as we have seen. They believed that a few divisions could leap across the Channel, seize a French port city by frontal attack, and then build up reinforcements. If they did not have the strength just then to advance upon Paris and the Rhine, they would certainly be able to pin down dozens of German divisions that might otherwise be deployed against the retreating Russians.

The British thought otherwise. They had greater respect for German military efficiency and power than did the Americans—respect they had gained through bitter experience. Furthermore, they remembered the costly bloodbaths of the First World War in northern France when frontal attacks had consumed hundreds of thousands of lives in a single day. They were certain that with the small forces then available, any Allied venture into France in 1942 was doomed to failure; and another failure, after a long string of defeats, might cost Churchill his political leadership of Great Britain.

The arguments between Allied leaders grew prolonged and bitter. The British, who had borne the brunt of the war so far, had to be careful not to estrange the Americans, for there were many American generals who would have gladly shifted their war effort to the conquest of Japan in the Pacific and abandoned the Europe-First strategy. Furthermore, Britain was utterly dependent upon American supplies of all kinds and, if hopes for final victory over Hitler were to be realized, American reinforcements in the millions. How could they convince the Americans that they were wrong?

Perhaps by going ahead with Jubilee on an enlarged scale —not simply as a commando raid, but as a full-scale frontal assault against Dieppe, which would be a rehearsal for the invasion of Europe. The British were sure that such an assault would prove a bloody failure, and that ought to convince the Americans that an invasion of Europe in 1942 or even 1943 was out of the question.

But to their surprise, with Roosevelt's support and the reluctant concurrence of General Marshall, the British won their argument in the spring of 1942. Operation Torch—the invasion of North Africa—was decided upon, and all plans for an invasion of France could be postponed for at least a year. So the political reason for mounting Jubilee had vanished. But now other considerations were brought forward.

Even though the Allies planned no assault on continental Europe in 1942, was it not important to convince Hitler that this was still a possibility, thereby pinning down German forces in the west? And would not Jubilee serve to mislead the Nazis as to Allied intentions in the Mediterranean? In fact, the operation could be used to cover the gathering of forces in England for the later descent on North Africa. So while political reasons faded, deception became a new justification for Jubilee. Ominously the motives for the operation had become thoroughly muddled. If its tactical purposes were to succeed, it must be cloaked in absolute secrecy; but if its strategic purposes were to be fulfilled, the Germans would have to at least suspect that some such operation was in the wind. A disaster was in the making.

In the late spring of 1942 the BBC began broadcasting alarming messages to France, warning that an invasion was imminent and even suggesting that French populations on the Channel coast had better evacuate. At the same time the RAF began appearing in great strength over French Channel ports, challenging the *Luftwaffe* to battle. And British Intelligence began spreading rumors and dropping hints all over Europe that a landing was to be expected that summer, especially in the Pas de Calais, the French Channel coast closest to England. All of this activity had its desired results: The Germans were brought into a very high state of readiness and expectancy along the Channel coast. Reinforcements were sent to various port towns and the *Luftwaffe* accepted the RAF's challenge, shooting down nearly one thousand Allied planes in the process.

Meanwhile, the Germans launched a deception campaign of their own. Field Marshal Gerd von Rundstedt, German commander-in-chief in Western Europe, instructed German intelligence officers to start spreading the word that ports in the Pas de Calais area, including Dieppe, were only lightly defended. Using French agents they knew to be in English employ, the Germans "leaked" the information that Dieppe, for instance, was garrisoned by only 1,400 low-grade troops of the 110th Infantry Division; actually it was held by 5,000 first-class soldiers and a complete *Panzer* division was stationed nearby. And through French agents in *their* employ they gained information that indicated that Dieppe itself would be the Allied target. Then, as if to make certain that the Germans knew they were coming, the British launched two small-scale commando attacks against a French light-house near Dieppe on the very eve of the main assault.

On the afternoon of August 18, 1942, some six thousand troops embarked in more than two hundred ships for the assault upon Dieppe. Nearly all of them were Canadians, and this, too, was a political decision. Canada had long since sent two divisions of well-trained, well-equipped soldiers to England, all of them first-rate fighting men and all of them volunteers for overseas duty. They had been idle for two years and were eager to show what they could do. The Canadian government was anxious for the prestige of battle and Churchill, under pressure from the Canadian prime minister, Mackenzie King, agreed.

Three days earlier, on August 15, German intelligence radio officers, listening to the flow of English wireless communications, had noticed a change in their patterns. A sudden radio silence followed that day. The German experts knew from past experience that this often presaged an attack. At the same time German cryptanalysts had broken one of the Royal Navy's codes and were able to report that a large-scale naval movement was in the offing. And finally, as if to ensure the doom of Jubilee, a German coastal convoy ran into one of the Canadian convoys crossing the Channel. A firefight broke out and the Germans were scattered—but not before the German convoy commander had managed to signal his headquarters. Immediately all German troops in the Pas de Calais area were placed in a "battle imminent" alert.

The veteran German troops in and around Dieppe had been in a high state of alert since August 1; some slept on the beaches. Many thousands of mines had been laid along the Dieppe waterfront, buildings had been torn down to give the defenders a better field of fire, other buildings had been wired for demolition, and the hillside caves around Dieppe had been converted into machine-gun and antitank gun nests.

In the false-dawn light of August 19 off the Dieppe coast, troop ships lowered their boats, filled with Canadian troops, into the Channel waters. After a short run to the shore, just as the landing craft touched the beaches, the cave-hidden machine-gun and antitank nests opened fire. Canadian war correspondent Ross Munro, who accompanied the troops, wrote, "We bumped on the beach and down went the ramp and out poured the first infantrymen. They plunged into about two feet of water and machine-gun bullets laced into them. Bodies piled up on the ramp. Some staggered to the beach and fell. . . . They had been cut down before they had a chance to fire a shot." Then, with a shattering roar, various buildings in Dieppe were blown up. Canadian tanks, rumbling out of their LST's (Landing ShipTanks) dug themselves deep into the sand of the beaches and were promptly destroyed by antitank guns. Most of the Canadians never got beyond those beaches, and many were killed even before they disembarked. German bombers roaring overhead managed to severely damage many of the merchant vessels and warships, despite the presence of swarms of RAF fighters.

By late afternoon on August 19 it was all over. The remnants of Jubilee retreated in confusion across the Channel and back to English ports. By 5:40 P.M. that day Field Marshal von Rundstedt was able to telegraph Hitler that "No armed Englishman remains on the continent." The attack had been a grisly failure. Its cost was frightful: Of the six thousand Canadians taking part, more than 68 percent became casualties—killed, wounded, or captured against a

German casualty list of only 600. The RAF lost 106 planes, the *Luftwaffe* only 46. More than 10 percent of the ships taking part had been sunk. Von Rundstedt's report to Hitler concluded with the words "They will not do it like this a second time."

Dieppe was a total, complete defeat, and under the strange circumstances surrounding Jubilee—the security leaks, the alerting raids, the fact that the operation was not canceled when it was completely obvious that the Germans must know it was coming—it must be regarded as a conscious sacrifice of the men involved. Was the sacrifice in vain? German radar and radio installations *were* captured and carried back to England by a small party of commandos during the raid; German forces, including several first-class divisions, *were* held away from the Russian front; the American skeptics *were* finally convinced that the Allies were in no way prepared to invade Northern Europe; and the tactical lessons were valuable. As Winston Churchill later wrote, "It shed revealing light on many shortcomings in our outlook. It taught us to build in good time various new types of craft and appliances . . . and that teamwork was the secret of success." Strategically the lesson of Dieppe was that the Allies could not expect to seize a French Channel port by direct assault, and that any invading armies would somehow have to bring a seaport with them—which, as we shall see, they did a year and a half later. Nonetheless, it is permissible to question why these lessons had to be learned at such a terrible price and to read with more than a little irony Churchill's final epitaph on Jubilee: "Honour to the brave who fell. Their sacrifice was not in vain."

If Allied commanders were willing to sacrifice thousands of combat troops for political and strategic purposes of which the victims had no conception, British intelligence chiefs were prepared to sacrifice individual secret agents in enemy territory with no more compunction. Of the dozens of stories of such sacrifices that emerged after the war, the tale of the British agent known as "Madeleine" was perhaps the most poignant and must stand symbolic for the rest.

"Madeleine" was the code name of a young, exotically beautiful, and highly talented woman named Noor Inayat Khan. Her first name meant "Light of Womanhood" and she was an Indian princess, the daughter of Inayat Khan, leader of the Sufi sect of Moslem mystics. She was born on New Year's Day, 1914, in the royal palace of the Kremlin in Moscow, where her parents were guests of Tsar Nicholas II. The approaching storms of the Russian Revolution forced her family to flee Moscow shortly after her birth and she was raised principally in France.

At the outbreak of war, in 1939, Noor was living in Paris, earning her living writing children's stories for French radio. Just before the Germans marched into Paris, Noor escaped to England, where she enlisted in the Women's Auxiliary Air Force (WAAF). While serving as a telegraph operator, Noor was called to the War Office, where she was asked if she would be willing to work in German Occupied France. She volunteered at once and found herself assigned to Special Operations Executive (SOE), Colonel Gubbins's spy outfit, which, it will be recalled, had been ordered to "set Europe ablaze."

The first question of many now arises: Why was she accepted by SOE? One of her training officers reported that she was: "A splendid, vague, dreamy creature, far too conspicuous—twice seen, never forgotten." Another officer remarked that she was "too emotional and impulsive to be suitable for employment as a secret agent." Yet another of her tutors in spy work wrote: ". . . no sense of security. She has an unstable and temperamental personality and it is very doubtful whether she is really suited to work in the field." Yet these and other unfavorable comments were overridden by Colonel Maurice Buckmaster, head of SOE's French Section.

The work for which she was being trained was to act as a radio operator for one of the several British spy networks in France. These networks, given such code names as "Jade Amicol," "Prosper," "Scientist," "Orator," and many others, were designed to ferret out German secrets, carry on reconnaissance in German-occupied territory, and from time to time perform acts of sabotage against German installations. London kept them supplied with money, arms, equipment, and new agents through nighttime air drops or landings at secret airfields throughout France. But the spy networks, unknown to their members, had yet another function. This was to misinform and mislead the Germans. This function would become paramount if the British suspected that a network had been penetrated by German counterintelligence, was being betrayed by one or more of its members, or if it collapsed. In other words, when a spy network was falling into German hands, the British would pretend not to know about it and continue sending information (false), money and guns (real), and replacement agents, who were thereby delivered directly into the cells of the *Gestapo*. Were agents, money, and supplies considered expendable by London in the interests of deceiving the Germans?

A vital part of this kind of deception was the so-called "Radio Game," in German known as *Funkspiel*. Allied radio operators, like Noor, who were dropped to spy networks behind enemy lines were trained to send very special signals on their sets to identify them and assure listeners in London that they were not under enemy control. Besides that, each radio operator had his or her own very personal way of handling a telegraph key—a way that could, like finger-prints, identify them to listeners familiar with their touch. But if the British suspected that a radio operator had fallen into German hands, or that the Germans were themselves using the operator's call letters and codes, they might never-theless continue to play the Radio Game, hoping thereby to use that channel to feed false information to the enemy. Of course, in order to convince the Germans that they still be-lieved signals were coming from their own operator, the British would have to go along with requests for arms, cer-tain kinds of true information, and, again, replacement agents. The Germans were themselves very expert at *Funk-spiel*, and this intricate game had depths of double and triple deception to the point of utter confusion.

Early in 1943, London began to suspect that its Prosper network in the Paris area had either been penetrated by German agents or harbored a traitor. Nonetheless, when Emil-Henri Garry, a French agent in Prosper, called for a replacement radio operator, Noor and two other women were secretly landed near the city of Le Mans on the night of June 16–17, 1943. Later it was said that the arrival of the three agents had been betrayed to the Germans by a French traitor in Prosper's employ and that it was even witnessed by German security agents hidden at the edge of the clandestine airfield. But none of this was ever proven.

Witnessed or not, the three women made their way to the

nearest railroad station, at the town of Angers. There they split up and Noor boarded a train for Paris. Her false identification papers got her past German guards both at Angers and Paris, and late on June 17 she arrived at Garry's home. There she admitted that she had eaten nothing since arriving in France because she was unsure of how to use her French food and restaurant ration coupons. And she presented Garry with a bouquet of carnations! The French agent who, by some strange omission had *not* been forewarned of her arrival, was appalled that London would send him so delicate and innocent an agent.

Nonetheless, Noor was accepted by Prosper, given lodgings near the Bois de Boulogne—not far from *Gestapo* headquarters on Avenue Foch—and began sending signals to London. She enlisted the help of her next-door neighbor, a German, to help her put up her aerial, which, she explained, was a clothesline.

But shortly after Noor's arrival in Paris, the entire Prosper network, betrayed by French traitors and thoroughly penetrated by German agents, began to collapse. Dozens of agents were arrested and carried off to *Gestapo* torture cells. Informed by Noor of Prosper's downfall, London ordered her home—some survivors of the network were being flown out secretly on the night of August 15—but she refused to leave her post until a replacement radio operator arrived.

Amazingly Noor survived in Paris for another two months. The Germans knew of her existence but not her whereabouts. She constantly kept moving so as to baffle German radio directional listening posts. But in mid-October 1943, Noor's address was sold to the Germans (for $2,400) by Garry's sister, Renée. Noor was immediately seized, as were her code books and other equipment, and carried off to *Gestapo* headquarters on Avenue Foch. There she was interrogated.

What the Germans wanted from Noor was the special information—her private code signals to London and intimate personal details—with which they could use her transmitter to open a game of *Funkspiel* with the British. But despite torture, Noor absolutely refused to give away anything to her captors. She even managed on two occasions to escape from the building on Avenue Foch, but was soon recaptured each time.

Even without Noor's cooperation the Germans reopened her link with London. British listeners were immediately suspicious because the style of the transmissions suggested that she was being impersonated. Nonetheless, so expert were the Germans at this game that London, at the false "Madeleine's" request, sent in drops of money, arms, and even agents—all delivered into German hands. But the question remains: Did the British know of this German trick and purposely sacrifice supplies and agents so that they could misinform the enemy? The great invasion of Europe was now, during the winter of 1943–44, barely six months off. If London could convince the Germans that landings would be made anywhere else than the Normandy peninsula (the real target), they might save the lives of hundreds of thousands of soldiers. On balance, what did the lives of a handful of secret agents—all volunteers for the most perilous of jobs —matter? Yet to this day the British government denies that it made such sacrifices. If so, then the high price in lives paid by the British in order to deceive the Germans about the time and place of D-Day must be ascribed to inefficiency, war-time confusion, accident, and German expertise.

Noor herself, after six weeks at Avenue Foch, was sent to a German prison in heavy chains. Her existence was as miserable and tortured as that of any concentration camp inmate. Eventually she was transferred to the infamous German camp at Dachau. There, on the morning of September 14, 1944, Noor and three other women agents of SOE were shot. Their corpses were burned.

Intentionally sacrificed or not, Princess Noor Inayat Khan was not forgotten by England. After the war, on April 5, 1949, she was posthumously awarded the George Cross for "acts of the greatest heroism and of the most conspicuous courage in circumstances of extreme danger." A plaque in her memory was placed in the wall of a London church, and there, every year, someone has left a small bunch of spring flowers.

The War Diary

January–June, 1944/U.S.–British air offensive wrecks *Luftwaffe*, gains absolute air supremacy over Europe.

June 5, 1944/Rome falls to Allied armies.

June 6, 1944/D-Day: Allies launch massive invasion of Western Europe through the Normandy Peninsula.

"TRUTH IS SO PRECIOUS . . ." 8

One has to be on the watch like a spider
in its web. Thank God I've always had
a pretty good nose for everything so
that I can generally smell things out
before they happen.

ADOLF HITLER

It was in the city of Teheran, Iran, in November 1943,
during one of the war-time conferences of the Big Three—
Churchill, Roosevelt, and Stalin—that Allied plans for the
invasion of Western Europe were explained to the Russians.
Much had happened in the preceding six months—the conquest of Sicily, the landing in Italy; Allied armies were now
slogging their way toward Rome against fierce German resistance, the collapse of Mussolini's Fascist regime, and the
Italian surrender. But though much had been won, more
remained to be gained. The invasion of Western Europe in
the face of German might was going to be—in the words of
the Duke of Wellington, speaking of the Battle of Waterloo
—"a close-run thing, a damned close-run thing—the closest-
run thing you ever saw in your life." If anyone doubted that,

the tragedy of Dieppe was still fresh in memory. And to keep from the Germans the three great secrets of D-Day—when, where, and how—the Allies had devised a mighty deception campaign code-named Operation Bodyguard, because, as Churchill remarked to Stalin, "In war-time, truth is so precious that she should always be attended by a bodyguard of lies."

The plans agreed upon by the Joint Chiefs of Staff committee meeting in Washington were to land a total of five divisions—two American, two English and one Canadian—on the eastern beaches of the Normandy peninsula in the first assault wave. This attack would be preceded by the nighttime dropping of one British and two American airborne divisions behind the coastal zone. The date fixed for the mighty invasion, which would be transported and covered by more than six thousand ships and ten thousand planes, was the first week in June 1944, when moon and tide conditions would be favorable. Since the landing troops were not expected to capture a port for some time, they would bring their ports with them in the form of giant concrete caissons that could be linked together to form mile-long piers. The piers themselves would be protected from harsh Channel seas by sinking miles of old freighters, Liberty ships for the most part, to form artificial harbors. Fuel would be delivered directly to the beachheads through PLUTO (Pipeline Under the Sea). By these means the Allies hoped to build up reinforcements and supplies in the danger zones quickly enough to hold off the expected German counterattack.

That attack, when it came, could be devastating. Against the first eight Allied divisions ashore—which included the paratroopers—Rommel, who was now in command in the west, could throw a total of twenty-five first-class *Wehr-*

macht divisions, including ten *Panzer* divisions. Five of these were already stationed in the Normandy area, the rest were concentrated mainly in the Pas de Calais. Bodyguard's principal objective was to keep those fifteen powerful divisions of the German Fifteenth Army pinned to their positions hundreds of miles from the battlefield and to persuade Hitler not to rush massive reinforcements to Normandy from such areas as the Balkans and the Russian front.

In order to achieve their aims, Bodyguard planners had to convince the Germans that the Allies were preparing powerful attacks against German positions in Greece and, in conjunction with the Russians, against Norway. Most improbably of all, they had to convince *der Führer* that the Normandy landings, when they came, were merely a diversionary thrust and that the real Great Invasion would follow in the Pas de Calais. Furthermore, true Allied plans—which were known in detail by hundreds of higher-ranking officers and which might be surmised from the many thousands of orders that must be issued to Allied armies, fleets, and air squadrons—had to be kept absolutely secret from the German high command. French Resistance forces had to be alerted in good time to prepare their essential blows against German communications, but could not be informed of the actual place and date of D-Day lest this information fall into German hands.

All real Allied operations in Northern Europe were given the code name Overlord, while the Normandy invasion itself was called Operation Neptune. Bodyguard's phony invasions were given the following code names: the attack on Greece was Operation Zeppelin, that on Norway was Fortitude North, a false landing in Southern France was called Operation Vendetta, an assault on the French Atlantic coast was named Operation Ironside, while the threat to the Pas de Calais region was Fortitude South. And behind each of these names, huge armies, fleets, and air forces had to be conjured into existence out of thin air, at least in German minds. Essentially the German general staff, as efficient and cunning a military organization as the world had ever known, must be tricked into abandoning what experience and military logic dictated: that the Allies would concentrate all their forces for a single massive blow and that this blow would fall on the perfectly obvious target area at the perfectly obvious time.

The first of Bodyguard's deceptions, Operation Zeppelin, got under way during the autumn of 1943 with a British attack upon the Greek Dodecanese islands of Cos, Samos, and Leros. This assault was not simply part of the Zeppelin fraud. It was hoped that success on the islands would persuade Turkey to join the Allies, and the islands themselves would provide air bases from which German positions in the Balkans could be more easily bombed. However, it would serve Zeppelin's purposes by focusing German attention on the threat from the eastern Mediterranean. In any event the British attacks were a failure. The Americans, opposed to British "adventures" so far from the main fighting fronts, refused to lend air support; the Germans reacted vigorously; and 6,000 British troops were marched off to Nazi prisoner-of-war camps. But from the viewpoint of Bodyguard planners the defeat did serve to excite German suspicions about Allied intentions in that area. To further rivet Hitler's attention to the Balkans, British Intelligence embarked on a complex spy game involving the German-employed agent who would become famous after the war as "Cicero."

Cicero was a Turk named Elyesa Bazna who was employed as a valet by Sir Hughe Knatchbull-Hugessen, British ambassador to Turkey, the elderly scion of an ancient and exceedingly aristocratic English family. Sir Hughe, known irreverently as "Snatch" to his Foreign Office colleagues, was a devotee of German *Lieder* (ballads), and Bazna had a fine tenor voice with which he would sing those mournful songs every day after lunch while Snatch accompanied him on the piano. In this way Bazna won Sir Hughe's admiration —and confidence.

It must not be thought that Sir Hughe, despite his Victorian manners and odd taste in music, was a dilettante. On the contrary, he was very effective in countering German influence in Turkey and highly diligent in his chief task, which was to persuade the Turks that the Allies would eventually win and that *now* was the time to join them. His ability and discretion were so highly regarded in London that he was kept very fully informed about Allied policy and plans. This information, in the form of documents and telegrams marked Secret and Most Secret, Sir Hughe was in the habit of bringing home to his residence, where he could read them at leisure. When he was not reading them they were kept locked in their original dispatch boxes.

This greatly simplified things for Bazna. The Turkish valet made a wax impression of Sir Hughe's key to the dispatch boxes, made a key from the impression, and in late October 1943 he removed some of the documents, photographed them with a 35-millimeter Leica camera, and then returned them to their boxes. A few days later he offered to sell the photographs to Ludwig Moyzisch, the head of German Intelligence in Turkey. Bazna's asking price for the first roll was £20,000 ($80,000).

Moyzisch immediately suspected an Allied plot to plant

false documents on him. Bazna claimed to have done his work entirely alone and only for the money he was demanding. But Bazna's efficiency, daring, and manners seemed to indicate that he must be a trained espionage agent. Furthermore, his description of the contents of the documents indicated that they were of such tremendous importance that Moyzisch could not imagine a British ambassador handling them so loosely. He consulted his superiors in Berlin. While German Foreign Minister Joachim von Ribbentrop and General Walter Schellenberg (Admiral Canaris's second-in-command) were also suspicious, they advised Moyzisch to proceed. Bazna was given his £20,000 and Moyzisch received a roll of 35-millimeter film.

When the film was developed and printed, both Moyzisch and higher authorities in Berlin were staggered. Internal evidence revealed that the documents were absolutely genuine and that they revealed the most highly-guarded Allied secrets, both military and political. While continuing to be suspicious of Bazna, the Germans were convinced of the authenticity of the material he provided and worked with him until April 1944, when Bazna resigned his post with Sir Hughe. The spy had been paid a grand total of £300,000 ($1.2 million) for his services.

The case of Cicero would, in the form of Bazna's memoirs and a subsequent film, become famous after the war as an example of British blundering in the field of espionage. How could such an obvious agent have been hired by Sir Hughe in the first place? It was known to British Intelligence that the man was a petty crook and had worked for both the Yugoslav and the German embassies in Turkey just prior to his being hired. There was even some information that hinted that Bazna had once been trained in espionage by the

Italian secret service. And if this was not enough, American counterespionage agents both in the German embassy in Ankara and in Berlin reported on Bazna's treachery to the British while it was going on. MI-6 told the Americans to mind their own business and Sir Hughe himself was never warned of his valet's activities.

Which was all according to plan. For although Bazna was a genuine crook, he played into the hands of the British. As Menzies himself said many years later, "Of course Cicero was under our control!" The vital information contained in those Most Secret documents Bazna turned over to the Germans was either not crucially important or was information the Germans might have gotten from other, public sources. But hidden among the dispatches and telegrams were hints that the Allies planned, with or without Turkish cooperation, to invade the Balkans in 1944. Hitler, to whom the documents were shown personally, began to pour reinforcements into the Balkans—a total of twenty-five divisions, including two *Panzer* divisions. There they remained, very far from Normandy, for the rest of the war. Any one of those divisions, launched against the beaches on D-Day, could have made the Allied invasion a disaster.

As for Bazna himself, after leaving Sir Hughe's employ he formed a construction company in Ankara with his ill-gotten loot. Unfortunately, however, the Germans had paid him in forged British bank notes. When the Turkish authorities found their banks flooded with phony British currency, Bazna was a ruined man; he nearly went to jail for fraud. After the war, for many years he eked out a poor living as a used-car salesman in Istanbul. In the late sixties he even brought a lawsuit against the West German government, demanding restitution for having been "swindled" by the

Nazis! But his claims were laughed off and he died a pauper in 1971. But not until 1975, when British Intelligence files were made public, did the Germans realize that their most famous agent, Cicero, was part of the many games British Intelligence played to guard the secrets of D-Day.

The British, however, did not always win these games. In fact they lost a very vital radio game to Josef Goetz, the German Intelligence radio expert stationed in Paris. It was Goetz who kept open the wireless links to London of captured British agents; it was he, in fact, who had impersonated "Madeleine" after she fell into *Gestapo* hands.

The game involved the so-called "personal messages" broadcast every night by the BBC to occupied Europe. These messages were words, sentences, and bits of poetry that were actually prearranged codes whose meanings were known only to the various spy networks to which they were addressed. For example, the words "Christmas is only twenty days away" might be an order to French Resistance units to blow up a certain bridge; "Pierre has fallen ill" might be notification to a spy network that a new agent would be parachuted in on a certain date. The BBC also broadcast many false and meaningless messages simply to confuse German listeners. In any event the individual codes could not be broken unless they were directly betrayed to the Germans.

Allied plans for D-Day involved a general uprising by French Resistance forces that would blow up bridges, roads, and railway lines; destroy German telephone networks; wreck power plants; and so forth. And it was through the BBC's "personal messages" system that the British intended to alert the French Underground. The code chosen was taken from a poem by Paul Verlaine, "Song of Autumn."

The BBC would broadcast the line "The long sobs of autumnal violins" as an alert two weeks before D-Day. This would be followed by the line "Soothe my heart with melancholy languor," which was the action message warning that D-Day would take place within the next forty-eight hours.

Now, after the capture of Madeleine and subsequently the capture of various other British radio operators, British Intelligence was fully aware that the Germans, through torture and betrayal, might well have pierced many of the "personal messages" codes, including the Verlaine poem. So it was planned to change all the codes just before D-Day. But just to further confuse the enemy, the BBC would broadcast the compromised codes as well as the new ones. Unfortunately someone forgot to change the Verlaine "personal message" and it remained perfectly valid. Josef Goetz was thus able to warn his superiors that "The first part of this signal . . . will be broadcast by the English radio on the first and fifteenth of given months, while the second part [will] . . . mean that the landings would ensue during the next forty-eight hours." The complications of bluff, counterbluff, and triple-bluff had grown so entangled that the British gave away one of the great secrets of the invasion, the date of D-Day; or rather, they placed the key to that date in German hands. What use the Germans would make of this key we shall soon see.

While the Germans were piecing together the meaning of the Verlaine poem, Allied preparations for Ironside and Vendetta, the false invasions of western and southern France, proceeded. Increasing diplomatic pressure was put on Turkey (and leaked to German agents) to join the Allies. The British Ninth and Tenth "Armies," which consisted of only a few thousand men each, gathered at the Turkish-

Syrian borders as if preparing to advance through Turkey to attack the Balkans. Diplomatic and newspaper leaks were orchestrated for German benefit from Washington to Ankara, from London to Algiers, all indicating an imminent Allied assault against Southern Europe. And in the case of Ironside the Double-Cross Committee, which controlled and manipulated captured German agents in Britain, went to work.

The Double-Cross Committee's key agent for Ironside was a young Argentinian woman who had been recruited by Canaris's *Abwehr* in Vichy France in 1942. She agreed to go to London for German Intelligence, but when she arrived she immediately informed MI-6 of her assignment. MI-6 turned her over to the Double-Cross Committee, who gave her the code name Bronx and in 1943 put her to work. She began writing invisible-ink letters to German agents in neutral Lisbon. As in the case of all double agents, the Double-Cross Committee kept her supplied with true but low-level intelligence, which the Germans could easily check out, until it was very certain that she had won German confidence. Then, in May 1944, she sent the following message to her bank, the Bank of the Holy Ghost, in Lisbon: "Send £50 quickly. I need it for my dentist." In the German code with which Bronx had been supplied this meant: "I am certain that the Allies will land on the Bay of Biscay coast in approximately one month." The Germans believed this message, and as a result the powerful German Eleventh *Panzer* Division was kept in the Bordeaux area, hundreds of miles from Normandy, until long after the invasion.

As part of the Vendetta orchestration, the reborn French army in North Africa, reequipped by the Americans, began amassing at Algerian ports as if in preparation for an invasion of Southern France. A dramatic increase in radio com-

munications between imaginary English and American headquarters and units also took place in North Africa. And to
provide icing for the deception cake, it was decided that
Field Marshal Bernard Montgomery ought to go to North
Africa in order to inspect these nonexistent forces. But of
course the real Montgomery was far too busy in Britain to
take time off, so a double was found. This was Lieutenant
Meyrick James, a clerk in the British army paymaster's
office in London. He was the spitting image of Montgomery
and, when dressed in a field marshal's uniform, could hardly
be told from the world-famous original. Unfortunately, unlike the real Montgomery, who was a strict teetotaler, James
was a heavy drinker. He managed to smuggle a hip-flask of
gin into his personal belongings, and when he arrived to
"inspect" British forces in Gibraltar, he was quite drunk.
Nonetheless, he was hurried through the ceremonious official
reception, attended by the governor of Gibraltar and all his
top aides at the airport, in plain view of Spanish and German
agents, and if anyone noticed that he staggered a bit, it was
put down to the rigors of his air trip. At Algiers, where he
was again met by all the top brass, "Monty" was quite sober
and, after a few days of very public inspection of French,
American, and British forces in North Africa, James was
returned to the obscurity of his real job in London. If the
Germans were ever fooled by the false Montgomery's presence at Gibraltar or in North Africa, there is no record of
the fact or that it influenced their tactical dispositions in any
way. They relied, it would seem, on other sources of information.

That information was supplied in abundance by the
Double-Cross Committee and the Resistance forces all over
Europe. From Norway to Greece a violent campaign of

sabotage now rose to whirlwind proportions. German trains were blown up, German communications cut, German soldiers murdered, factories and public utilities put out of action, all to create not only the appearance of imminent assault far from Normandy, but also to generate fear among Hitler's troops, to convince them that they were surrounded by stealthy enemies who might strike at any time. Paralyzed by confusion, the German high command, at Hitler's insistence, kept their occupation forces in place so as to be ready to meet any threat from any direction.

The primary deception of Bodyguard, however, was Fortitude South, the false invasion of the Pas de Calais area. This assault was to be carried out by FUSAG (First United States Army Group), a wholly imaginary force under the command of General George S. Patton, "Old Blood and Guts" himself, whose brilliant exploits in North Africa and Sicily had already won him recognition among the Germans as the ablest of Allied commanders. It seemed only logical to the German general staff that no matter under whose command other landings might be made, the main invasion would certainly be Patton's. But without strict adherence to military logic, none of Bodyguard's deceptions would have worked. Thus it was perfectly logical that the Allies would make diversionary landings in the Balkans, Southern and Western France, Norway, and even on the French Channel coast to tie down German reinforcements. It was also logical that when the main attack came it would follow the shortest route, Dover to Calais, and land in the most dangerous territory, the Belgian coast, from which an invading army might immediately threaten the German industrial complex in the Ruhr Valley.

To reinforce that logic, British and American Intelligence conjured up a huge army in southeastern England. All the old tricks were employed, involving inflatable tanks and trucks and artillery pieces—this time by the hundreds of thousands—the laying of false tank tracks, the creation of phony ammunition dumps. Hundreds of air patrols were flown to protect the FUSAG concentration from German aerial reconnaissance, but not protect it too well. Patton himself was conspicuous in the area on endless inspection tours. Vastly increased radio activity was broadcast in the area, and local people were even persuaded to write letters to the editors of local newspapers protesting the invasion of their farms and towns by hordes of American and British troops. In ports around Dover hundreds of landing craft, each nothing more than scaffolding and canvas floating on empty oil drums, were concentrated. Among the false radio messages exchanged between FUSAG units was one that has become a classic: "Queen's Royal Regiment report a number of civilian women, presumably unauthorized, in the baggage train. What are we going to do with them—take them to Calais?" And while the real PLUTO (Pipeline Under the Sea) was being prepared opposite Normandy, a phony pipeline was being constructed at Dover, along with a huge oil dock. The king himself, along with Montgomery and Eisenhower, "inspected" this installation and made speeches to the "construction workers" involved.

But the crowning touch to FUSAG was provided by no less trustworthy a personage than General Hans Cramer, former commander of the *Afrika Korps*, who had been captured by the Allies in Tunisia. Since the general's health was none too good, it had been decided to return him to Germany through an exchange program run by the Swedish Red Cross. But before he left England, British Intelligence put him to work for Bodyguard. They did this by driving the general in a command car to his embarkation port on the North Sea. His trip was leisurely and was routed through the FUSAG area. There, in passing, he saw huge concentrations of tanks, artillery, supplies of all kinds. He had dinner with Patton (who was introduced as "Commander in Chief, FUSAG") and conversations with several divisional commanders, all of whom talked of the coming landings near Calais.

Now, while conversations might have been misleading, no German general could have been fooled by dummy preparations. So General Cramer was driven through the real invasion concentration areas. The tanks, troops, and artillery and supply dumps he saw were all very real. But he was told that he was in the Dover region, and since all signposts and place-names on roads and in villages had long since been removed, the general had no way of knowing that his drive had been through south-central England, a long way from the FUSAG area.

When General Cramer finally reached Germany he made detailed reports to the general staff of all he had seen and heard—and *where* he had seen and heard it. Cramer's reports—he made one personally to Hitler—were accepted without question, for who would doubt the word of a German general? Hitler was absolutely convinced that the main Allied thrust, when it came, would hit the Pas de Calais region. And if some German generals, lacking *der Führer's* remarkable "military intuition," were not yet totally convinced, they were at least doubtful, so that their protests at Hitler's troop dispositions were not too strenuous.

Actually Field Marshal Erwin Rommel, now in command of German forces in France, did not intend to be distracted. His plan was simplicity itself: He would hold back the most powerful German armored divisions as a reserve. When the Allied invasion came—wherever it came—it would quickly be obvious whether it was or was not the main thrust. Just as soon as the question was resolved—a matter of hours— Rommel intended to throw his reserves directly against the beachheads and drive the Allies back into the sea. He figured that he had three days in which to launch this counterattack; after that time the Allied buildup of reinforcements would be too great to be dislodged. There was only one catch to the plan: Rommel was not in direct command of the reserve German divisions in the west. That command was vested in Hitler personally and no division would move one inch without direct orders from *der Führer*. Through Ultra, Allied Intelligence was well aware of this.

If the Germans remained ignorant of exactly where the blow would fall, they were also ignorant of when it would fall, despite German Intelligence's penetration of the Verlaine poem system. For the first line of that poem had been broadcast on May 1, and on that occasion Field Marshal von Rundstedt had indeed alerted all his forces, only to see that nothing came of it. When the line was repeated on June 1, the Germans paid no attention, and when the action section of the code—the second line of the poem—was broadcast on June 5, it was also ignored.

What was decisive in persuading the Germans that there would be no Allied invasion on June 6 was the state of the weather. The German high command knew as well as the Allies that large-scale landings could only take place during certain conjunctions of moon and tide and that one such conjunction would occur from June 3 to June 7. But their weather experts reported high gales and stormy waves in the Channel during those days, and indeed, German commanders could see those conditions for themselves. What they did not know was that the weather would calm down during June 6 and 7—a brief lull between storms. The reason they did not know this was because Allied patrols had destroyed all the secret German weather stations posted in Greenland in a savage little war fought above the Arctic Circle. So confident were the Germans that the weather precluded an invasion during the first week of June that Rommel left his command to make a visit to Germany: He wanted to persuade Hitler to release those reserve divisions to his direct command.

So, on June 6, 1944, Allied paratroopers rained from the skies over Normandy, and a few hours later the great Allied armadas began landing their troops on the beaches under the protective fire of hundreds of warships and the air cover of thousands of planes. Although local German commanders were alerted by these events, it was now too late for the German high command to rush reinforcements to meet the Allies on the beaches, but not too late for Rommel's counterblow to be struck, if only *der Führer* would give him the necessary reserves.

Through Ultra, London was able to "listen" to the German arguments as they were in progress. And by D-Day plus two, it seemed that Rommel had won. The heavy German armored divisions of the Fifteenth Army, stationed in the Pas de Calais, were to be sent to Normandy. If and when they arrived they would make mincemeat of the still-gathering Allied forces on their modest beachheads. This was the crisis point for Bodyguard; so far the plan had worked admirably to befuddle the enemy, but now, with the solid evidence of the invasion of Normandy before their very eyes, it seemed that the Germans could be fooled no longer.

No longer? Perhaps just one more time. The "violins,"

as they were called in spy parlance, with which British Intelligence intended to complete the orchestration of Fortitude South, were two German agents code-named Garbo and Brutus. Both were in the employ of MI-6 and both for many months had been broadcasting from England, under MI-6 control, such "secrets" as London wanted German Intelligence listeners to hear. Garbo's real name remains a mystery to this day. All that is known of him is that he was probably Spanish, that he hated Nazism and Communism equally, and that from 1942 on he was under the direct orders of the Double-Cross Committee. More, but not much more, is known about Brutus. He was Captain Roman Garby-Czerniaski, a member of the Polish general staff who escaped to Paris when Poland was overrun by the *Wehrmacht* in 1939. He stayed behind after the fall of France and became a British agent. He was betrayed to the Germans, however, and sent off to prison to await execution. But the Germans were looking for potential agents at that time to infiltrate British Intelligence. His German captors made Garby-Czerniaski an offer: If he would work for them, then one hundred of the French Resistance agents who had been captured with him would be treated as prisoners of war rather than as spies. Their lives, in other words, would be spared. Garby-Czerniaski agreed. His "escape" from German hands was arranged, and in January 1943 he finally arrived in London. Of course, he immediately went to work as a double agent for the Double-Cross Committee and, like Garbo, transmitted to Germany enough factual information to win the confidence of German Intelligence. The Resistance agents were shot anyway.

Now, in the hours following D-Day, was the time to use both Garbo and Brutus—while Allied forces were holding on to their beachheads desperately and bracing for a blow that, if it came on time, would drive them back into the sea. On June 8, 1944, just two days after D-Day, Brutus broadcast to his German patrons in Paris that he had "seen with [his] own eyes the Army Group Patton [FUSAG] preparing to embark at east-coast and southeastern English ports." Brutus added that FUSAG would have some fifty divisions available for the new landing, which obviously would hit the Pas de Calais area. And on June 9 Garbo broadcast a general review of Allied forces poised to make a second landing on the Continent. "I transmit this report," he said, "with the conviction that the present assault is a trap. . . ."

To lend credence to these reports, Allied air forces pounded the coastal areas of Belgium while light naval forces bombarded certain Belgian Channel ports. Transport planes dropped hundreds of "paratroopers"—which were actually dummies—but since they had done just that to mislead German patrols during the *real* paratroop invasion in Normandy on the night of June 5–6, the Germans concluded that a new airborne invasion was imminent.

All this information regarding Allied demonstrations off the Pas de Calais, as well as the Garbo and Brutus messages, was transmitted immediately to Hitler's headquarters. There *der Führer* came to his decision. The Normandy landings were, he told his generals, a gigantic Allied ruse to lure German divisions away from the scene of the real invasion, which would take place along the Belgian coast. Not only were German forces forbidden to reinforce the Normandy defenses, they were transferred to the Fifteenth Army in Belgium. Hitler's decision almost brought about the resignations of von Rundstedt and Rommel, who knew the battle and hence the war was lost if they could not use their reserves to destroy the Allied Normandy landings immediately. But *der Führer's* intentions, made known through Ultra intercepts, brought elation to Allied leaders in London. As Lieutenant Colonel Sir Ronald Wingate, a member of the LCS, would recall, "We knew then that we'd won—there might be very heavy battles, but we'd won."

Bodyguard was a complete success in every area. Powerful German forces were deployed in the Balkans, along the French Mediterranean coast, on the Bay of Biscay near Bordeaux, and in Belgium—sufficient forces to have overwhelmed the Normandy beachheads in a matter of hours. But they were chained to their positions far from the battlefield through the tricks and stratagems of Vendetta, Zeppelin, Ironside, Fortitude North, and Fortitude South. It was the crowning achievement of Allied Intelligence during the war and the justification of all the sacrifices made during previous months and years.

For Wingate was right: There would be heavy battles ahead, but the war was won as soon as the Allies established themselves permanently in France. So obvious was this to the Germans themselves that just six weeks after D-Day the *schwarze Kapelle,* the German anti-Hitler underground, attempted to assassinate *der Führer* and end the war. They failed and paid with their lives—Admiral Canaris being but one of hundreds of victims of Hitler's vengeance—and the war went on for another ten months, but after June 6, 1944, its outcome was never in doubt.

The War Diary

June 9, 1944/Germans launch first V rockets against England.

July 20, 1944/German officers attempt to kill Hitler and end the war. Their plot fails.

August 15, 1944/Allies invade Southern France.

August 25, 1944/Paris liberated.

September 7, 1944/Belgium liberated; Allied forces stand on German border.

December 16, 1944/Germans attack U.S. forces; Battle of the Bulge begins.

January 2, 1945/Battle of the Bulge ends in German defeat.

January 11, 1945/Russians commence huge offensive in Poland. Warsaw falls.

February 2, 1945/Russians fifty miles from Berlin.

March 7, 1945/Allied armies reach and cross the Rhine River.

April 12, 1945/President Roosevelt dies in Warm Springs, Georgia.

April 25, 1945/American and Russian forces meet at Torgau in central Germany. Berlin besieged by Russians.

April 30, 1945/Adolf Hitler commits suicide in Berlin.

May 2, 1945/Germans surrender in Italy; Mussolini executed in Milan.

May 7, 1945/Germany surrenders unconditionally; war in Europe ends.

APOCALYPSE NOW 9

Although personally I am quite content
with the existing explosives, I feel we must
not stand in the path of improvement . . .

WINSTON CHURCHILL

The bomb was exploded about 2,000 yards above London's
crowded East End dock area at precisely ten minutes after
midnight. Instantly a huge fireball formed with the bright-
ness of a miniature sun; those who looked upon it were
permanently blinded. The tremendous heat generated by
this fireball incinerated human beings within a one-mile
radius and set buildings afire two miles away. Soon a tremendous fire storm would consume half of the great British
metropolis. The blast that, within seconds, followed the
appearance of the fireball, flattened every structure within
10,000 yards of the epicenter; Parliament, Westminster
Abbey, Buckingham Palace, the Thames bridges—all were
utterly destroyed. During the first minute of disaster more
than 300,000 Londoners were killed; some 200,000 more

perished within the next few hours, and in succeeding months and years many thousands more would die of a mysterious radiation poisoning.

At the same moment that the world's first atomic bomb hit London, another was exploded directly above the Kremlin in Moscow, with similar results.

Within hours after these twin disasters, Berlin's Radio Deutschland broadcast der Führer's message to the world. Stripped of its hysterical gloating and boasting, it amounted to this: All Russian armies were to retreat at once to the Ural Mountains, which separate Europe from Asia, pending the unconditional surrender of the Soviet government. Allied forces in Europe were to retreat into the Normandy peninsula, where they would be disarmed by German troops and led into prisoner-of-war cages. The British and American governments would immediately send representatives to Paris, where German peace terms would be dictated to them. Because French, Belgian, and Dutch Underground forces had co-operated with Allied troops in the west, every third citizen of those countries would be arrested and transported to certain "resettlement sites" in Poland. Although the first two atomic bombs had exploded over London and Moscow, the Americans need not think themselves immune: German long-range Dornier bombers, operating from Norway, were prepared to incinerate New York, Washington, and other American East Coast cities within hours. Unless Germany's enemies accepted der Führer's magnanimous terms, other cities in Britain, Russia, and the United States would be wiped out until not one stone was left standing upon another anywhere outside Germany. And now the great Nazi plan for the purification of the human race could begin. . . .

Such was the nightmare which sometimes disturbed the

sleep of a handful of Allied leaders during World War II—a handful, including Roosevelt, Churchill, Stephenson, the intelligence chiefs, and a few dozen scientists, because atomic research was the most highly guarded secret in the free world. The possibility of constructing nuclear bombs had been known to Allied scientists since 1939, and they had warned their respective governments that in this field Germany was at least as far advanced as any other country. It will be recalled that Britain's research into nuclear weapons had been turned over to the Americans during the summer of 1940. Further joint Anglo-American research would be carried out in the United States under the code-name Manhattan Project. But would free-world scientists beat the Germans in this dreadful race? No one could be sure.

Since the time of William Stephenson's secret trip in early 1940 through northern Norway, during which he persuaded Professor Leif Tronstad, the Norwegian manager of the Norsk Hydro heavy-water plant, to turn over the facility's blueprints, much had happened. Germany had conquered Norway and was in possession of Norsk Hydro itself and of the heavy water it produced, an essential ingredient in German atomic research. The plant's output had been increased under German control. If this was not in itself sinister enough news, worse had come from Dr. Niels Bohr, the great Danish physicist who was continuing atomic research in his laboratory in Copenhagen under German occupation. It seemed that in October 1941, Dr. Bohr had received a visit from Professor Werner Heisenberg, the leading German atomic scientist, and developer of quantum theory. Heisenberg wanted to know if Bohr felt it morally correct for a physicist to take part in the production of an atomic bomb. Bohr, a convinced pacifist, declared himself utterly opposed to it—but was such a bomb possible? Yes, Heisenberg said, it was not only possible but probable. The results of this alarming interview were smuggled to London by the "Princes," the Danish Underground organization, and MI-6 knew it had to act at once.

Professor Tronstad himself had escaped to England when the Nazis overran Norway and was now acting as chief of Norwegian secret-service operations in London. Menzies outlined MI-6's plans to Tronstad and the professor located one of his operatives, a man named Einar Skinnerland, who was a native of Rjukan, a small town near the Norsk Hydro plant. Skinnerland was parachuted onto the desolate Hardanger Plateau above Rjukan in March 1941. There, in the icy, snowbound wasteland, he was to establish an intelligence post. Skinnerland soon made contact with Norsk Hydro's chief engineer, Jomar Brun, who supplied him with detailed photographs of the plant, along with drawings of the German defense posts around it. All this material was microphotographed and smuggled by Skinnerland in a tube of toothpaste to Sweden, from where it was sent to London via diplomatic pouch.

Studying Skinnerland's photos and plans, Menzies and other Allied Intelligence chiefs decided that the only way to interrupt the German supply of heavy water from Norsk Hydro was to destroy the plant itself. And since such a task was beyond the resources of the Norwegian Underground, a full-scale commando attack would have to be launched from Britain. The code name for the operation was to be Freshman. Two teams of paratroopers—some forty men in all—would be landed by gliders on the Hardanger Plateau. There they were to contact Skinnerland and then storm the Norsk Hydro plant and blow it up.

Bad luck attended Operation Freshman from the beginning. The first party of paratroopers landed on October 18, 1942, unobserved by the Germans. But the second, main party ran into heavy storms over the Hardanger Plateau and their gliders crash-landed. The survivors of this disaster were quickly captured by German ski patrols, and after interrogation all were executed. Now the Germans were alerted to the danger to Norsk Hydro, and their defenses of the plant were greatly strengthened.

But Norsk Hydro still had to be destroyed, no matter what the cost, and a second attack, code-named Gunnerside, was prepared in Britain. Volunteers for this suicidal mission were recruited from Royal Norwegian Army units in England and trained in Scotland using an exact replica model of the Norsk Hydro plant as their target. Like the unfortunate Freshman team, they would land in gliders upon the Hardanger Plateau. There they would make contact with Skinnerland and the first Freshman party, now code-named Swallows. Then, instead of attempting to simply storm Norsk Hydro in the face of the greatly increased German defenses, which included artillery and machine-gun posts, the Gunnerside teams were to sneak into the plant under cover of darkness and blow up the eighteen stainless-steel concentration cells, huge vats that were essential to heavy-water production.

The Gunnerside men landed amid a raging blizzard on the Hardanger Plateau on February 16, 1943, and made their way across the barren ice fields twenty-eight miles to the Swallows hideout. There they found the survivors of Freshman, half-starved, ragged near-skeletons holed up in ice caves. Ten days later the combined teams made their way to the lip of the plateau, which overlooked the steep gorge in which the Norsk Hydro plant lay. Late at night on February 27 the men carefully clambered down the sides of the gorge, threading their way in the darkness through German mine-fields and past German sentry posts. They got into the plant itself through a cable duct, crawling one man at a time be-neath the powerfully humming plant generators. Then they carefully placed their explosive charges around each of the eighteen concentration cells, made their way out of the plant through the same cable duct, and were halfway up the side of the gorge when eighteen mighty explosions rent the night's silence. They made good their escape in the resultant confu-sion, embarked on a 250-mile march across the top of Nor-way, and eventually found safety in Sweden. Not a shot had been fired, not a life lost. The Germans had never even seen the Gunnerside attackers and Norsk Hydro had been put out of action. Allied Intelligence in London was satisfied that it would take the Germans two years to repair the damage.

Allied Intelligence was wrong: industrious German en-gineers had Norsk Hydro producing heavy water again within sixty days.

Meanwhile, Niels Bohr had reached a painful decision. The stout (he was affectionately nicknamed the Elephant) and genial Danish physicist, in whose Copenhagen labora-tory so much vital atomic research was conducted, had been wrestling with his conscience for a long time. He was, as we have said, a pacifist of deep conviction who felt that the unleashing of atomic weapons upon the world would consti-tute a moral crime of the first magnitude. Furthermore, en-grossed in his research, Bohr had little patience with or understanding of politics. He believed in the innate goodness of man, even Nazi man, and tended to dismiss reports of Hitler's savagery as Allied propaganda. In this he was aided by German policy toward Denmark. True, the Germans had conquered and occupied that tiny nation in the spring of 1940. But thereafter they had remained on their best behavior, especially toward Dr. Bohr, the value of whose work they well understood. German troops and administrators in Copenhagen kept a low profile and Denmark's King Christian X remained unmolested in his palace. The German iron fist was well concealed within a velvet glove.

But Dr. Bohr's continuing residence under Nazi rule undermined the Allied cause in two ways: First of all, it was always possible that the Germans would seize both the good doctor and his laboratory, thereby making a giant stride in their atomic research; secondly, British and American scientists needed Dr. Bohr in the United States to work on the Manhattan Project. But to entreaties from Allied agents and from Danish Underground workers that he take himself and his vital papers to England, Dr. Bohr turned a deaf ear.

Then, in September 1943, the Nazi occupiers of Denmark struck. Their principal targets were Denmark's 9,000 Jews. In order to round them up for shipment to the extermination camps in Poland, it was necessary to drop the mask of civility behind which Germany had ruled the country—necessary because the Danish people, from the king down to the humblest fisherman, absolutely refused to cooperate with German anti-Jewish measures. So the dreaded Nazi SS troops took over Danish police stations and even stormed King Christian's palace—1,000 "supermen" armed with machine guns and grenades overpowering the king's fifty royal guards armed with ceremonial swords. King Christian at once sent word to Dr. Bohr, advising him to flee the country. Bohr had time only to bury his most secret papers in the garden of his home at Carlsberg and then make his way to the coast, where he embarked on a small boat, part of the remarkable flotilla on which the Danish people carried almost all Denmark's Jews to safety in neutral Sweden.

Bohr reached Sweden on the last day of September 1943. Shortly after his arrival he was contacted by British agents, who offered to fly him to England. Although the agents refrained from mentioning the Anglo-American atomic bomb project for which his help was badly needed, Bohr surmised what lay behind their anxiety. Once again he protested his pacifist beliefs, but in view of the wave of Nazi terror that was now engulfing his homeland, he agreed to go.

So, on October 7, 1943, Dr. Bohr was taken to an abandoned airstrip near Stockholm. There he was bundled into a flight suit and placed in the empty bomb bay of a twin-engine Mosquito fighter-bomber painted black. This plane was one of many that comprised the so-called Moon Squadron of aircraft that slipped through German air defenses on special missions all over Europe. Mosquitoes were constructed largely of plywood to baffle German radar screens, and they flew at very high altitudes so that pilot and passenger both required oxygen masks. There was a communication link between the pilot and the bomb bay, but shortly after Bohr's plane took off from Sweden, this communication link failed. Worse than that, the oxygen supply to Dr. Bohr, sealed as in a coffin beneath the pilot's compartment, was faulty. When the Mosquito landed in England two hours after takeoff and the bomb bay was opened, Dr. Bohr was found unconscious inside. He was rushed to a nearby hospital and there revived. A few minutes more aboard the Mosquito and the world's greatest atomic scientist would have arrived in the free world dead.

The news that Dr. Bohr brought from Denmark was alarming. Not only were the Germans stepping up their heavy-water imports from Norway, but now they were stockpiling uranium, the key ingredient for an atomic bomb. While Dr. Bohr reluctantly joined his fellow scientists in the United States to work on the Manhattan Project, Allied Intelligence chiefs in London pondered the problem. In mid-November 1943 the American Eighth Air Force, based in Britain, made a large-scale precision-bombing attack on the Norsk Hydro plant near Rjukan. But although more than 700 heavy bombs were dropped, the plant escaped undamaged. Nonetheless, so much destruction was wrought in the area that the Germans decided to evacuate all the key Norsk Hydro facilities to Germany itself. This decision was known to London through Ultra almost as soon as it was reached.

Considering the time it would take the Germans to put the resettled plant into operation, and Germany's dwindling hydroelectric power sources, intelligence analysts in Britain considered that the evacuation of the plant itself presented little danger. But the transport to Germany of the fourteen tons of heavy water, in various stages of concentration, available at Rjukan would be very dangerous indeed. That much heavy water might be all the Germans needed to succeed in their atomic research. At the end of January 1943 Skinnerland, still operating his spy post on the Hardanger Plateau, radioed that the Norsk Hydro heavy water, stored for shipment in thirty-nine drums marked "Potash Lye," were ready for transport. The drums would be transported in a special freight train guarded by SS troops from the Norsk Hydro plant to the railroad ferry that crossed Lake Tinnsjö. On the other side of the lake the freight cars would once again be formed into a train and then proceed to a coastal port for loading onto ships bound for Germany. The entire route would be heavily guarded by elite SS units.

There was only one place at which the heavy-water consignment could be destroyed, and that was aboard the ferry-boat crossing Lake Tinnsjö. But since many Rjukan workers took that same ferry every day, many innocent lives would be lost. Skinnerland reported these facts to London with an urgent plea to the Norwegian government in exile to give its permission for the attack—urgent because the Germans planned to load the freight cars aboard the ferry for shipment across Lake Tinnsjö within a week, on Sunday, February 20. Here again was the moral problem: Skinnerland planned to blow up the ferry as it crossed the deepest part of the lake. Sinking it would entail the killing of many of its crew and passengers—men, women, and children—a sacrifice to the Allied war effort in which they would not be consulted. Weighing the awful scales of life and death, the Norwegian government ordered Skinnerland to proceed.

The Lake Tinnsjö ferry was an old, screwdriven boat named the *Hydro*. On the night of February 19 Skinnerland and a couple of his Norwegian agents boarded the ferry as it lay at its quay in Rjukan. The crew was having a party and there were no German guards aboard. But Skinnerland and his agents were stopped and questioned by a Norwegian watchman. They told him that they were on the run from the Germans and wanted to hide in the *Hydro*'s bilge. He agreed and showed them the way. When he had left them in the dark hold of the ship, Skinnerland and his men placed a sixteen-pound package of plastic explosive in the *Hydro*'s bow. This was wired to a simple alarm clock that would detonate the explosive exactly thirty minutes after the *Hydro* had left her dock the following morning. The agents' work was done by 4:00 A.M. and they silently crept from the boat. Then they made their way back to the Hardanger Plateau and from there traveled by ski, car, and train to Sweden.

At precisely 8:00 A.M. on the morning of Sunday, February 20, long before Skinnerland's men left Norwegian soil, the freight train carrying the heavy water left its siding next to the Norsk Hydro plant on its journey down to the ferry. SS guards swarmed over the train and were posted every thirty yards along the track. Overhead, light German reconnaissance planes guarded against any possible ambush. By 10:00 A.M. the freight cars were aboard the ferry and the *Hydro* set out across the lake with fifty-three passengers and crewmen aboard. Exactly on schedule, at 10:45 A.M., a tremendous explosion ripped off the bow of the boat. Within a few minutes the *Hydro* and its cargo sank into thirteen hundred feet of water with the loss of twenty-six of the people aboard. The price in innocent lives was high, but with the loss of Norsk Hydro's heavy water, German atomic research was decisively crippled.

The atomic bomb, although the most frightful, was not the only new weapon that Hitler was preparing to unleash upon the world. There were also long-distance rockets, primitive but effective guided missiles that *der Führer* planned to rain upon England in revenge for the air bombardment of German cities. Called V (for Vengeance) weapons, they were expected not only to bring Britain to ruin, but also to interrupt and destroy the Allied forces massing in England for the cross-Channel invasion of Europe. Yet despite Hitler's propaganda boasts about "decisive secret weapons," Allied Intelligence chiefs were at first quite skeptical as to their actual existence. "Secret weapons" might well be simply part of the old Nazi fear tactic that they used to demoralize their enemies.

It was not until March of 1943 that MI-6 learned that the V weapons were frighteningly real. It happened that during that month two German generals of the *Afrika Korps* who were captured in Tunisia, Hans Cruewell and Wilhelm von Thoma, were brought to London for interrogation. Between interviews with British Intelligence officers, von Thoma and Cruewell were left alone in a room wired for sound. During one of these "rest periods," MI-6 listeners heard von Thoma express surprise that London was not already in ruins from rocket bombardment. *Rocket* bombardment? MI-6 officials hastily dug out reports they had been receiving from French and Belgian agents about mysterious constructions being completed by the Germans in the Pas de Calais area. These were large underground galleries with steel tube tracks emerging from them, all aimed at London. Rocket launching sites?

On April 11, 1943, Menzies put all the evidence together in a memorandum, which he submitted to Churchill. It appeared that the German rocket threat was more than a mere boast: Reports from agents confirmed the construction of launching sites, and now Polish Underground workers reported that German experiments with long-range missiles were being conducted on a small island in the Baltic named Peenemünde. Ultra intercepts from German radar units on the Baltic coast, which were tracking experimental missile flights, gave further performance details of the new weapons. To confirm all this, early in 1943 the MI-6 station chief in Lisbon had been handed a mass of documents by a German officer—probably Captain Ludwig Gehre, an undercover agent in Admiral Canaris's *Abwehr* and a member of the *schwarze Kapelle*—regarding Germany's war effort. Known as the Lisbon Report, it included much secret information about Hitler's rocket program. There were, it seemed, two different V weapons under construction. One, the V-1, was a shorter-range (200 miles), stubby, winged missile that carried a 500-pound explosive payload at a speed of about 200 miles per hour. The other, the V-2, was a much larger, longer-ranged (500 miles) wingless missile that would descend at great speed (1,000 m.p.h.) from the stratosphere with a one-ton payload. Scientists and research facilities to develop these weapons were indeed located at Peenemünde. Hitler had promised his generals that the first V-1's would descend on London during October 1943.

All during the summer and fall of 1943 the RAF and the U.S. Eighth Air Force pounded every suspicious installation site along the Pas de Calais and every factory that was suspected of producing rocket parts. This aerial assault culminated on the night of August 17–18, when the RAF struck at Peenemünde itself. After drawing off German night fighters with a diversionary raid on Berlin, three waves of British heavy bombers roared in over the Baltic Island just 7,000 feet above the sea, dropping nearly 2,000 tons of high-explosive and incendiary bombs. Almost all the research facilities at Peenemünde were wrecked beyond repair and more than 730 German technicians and scientists vital to the rocket program were killed. Many more were badly wounded.

Hitler ordered the evacuation of all who survived the raid, transferring personnel and research equipment to Blizna, a small town near Cracow in Poland, while the actual manufacturing of the V missiles was transferred to a huge underground factory buried so deeply beneath the Harz Mountains in southern Germany that it was proof against any weight of bombs. The air offensive and the Peenemünde raid severely disrupted German missile production, but it did not stop it.

The first salvos of V-1's hit London on June 12, 1944, just six days after D-Day. Thereafter they would rain upon the British capital daily. More than 10,000 of these rockets were launched against England, and some 2,500 reached their targets. More than 6,000 civilians were killed and nearly 1.5 million English houses were destroyed. Defense against the V-1 was based upon its relatively slow speed— slow enough at 250 miles per hour to be hit by antiaircraft guns and even slow enough for Allied fighter planes to slip their wings beneath the missile's stubby fins and flip it off course. But when, in September 1944, the giant V-2's came plunging down from the stratosphere, there was no defense.

No defense but, perhaps, diversion. For the Germans had no way of knowing exactly where their V missiles were falling except through the reports of secret agents. As we have seen, these were all under control of the Double-Cross Committee. Garbo, Brutus, and others were put to work immediately. They reported to their German listening posts that the V-1's (and later the V-2's) were falling north of London. In response the Germans shortened the range of their missiles just enough so that instead of hitting the center of the city, most fell on the south London working-class districts. Once again Allied Intelligence and political leaders, especially Churchill, were called upon to play God. They could indirectly determine the "fall zone" for these terrible weapons, but even when they were diverted so as to miss London altogether, civilians elsewhere would die. Yet in

London was the cortex, the central nervous system of the entire Allied war effort against Hitler. It was decided to protect this vital area at the expense of death and destruction elsewhere.

The real miracle of the V-weapon campaign was that Hitler, in his blind fury and his lust for revenge, directed it against civilian targets. Had those missiles been launched against Allied military concentration areas in England— which were pouring reinforcements of men and equipment across the Channel to Normandy—or against the D-Day beachheads themselves, there might have been a military disaster of the first magnitude. Eventually the menace of the V rockets was extinguished when, during the late summer and fall of 1944, Allied armies broke out of the Normandy peninsula and swept across Europe to the Rhine, thereby overrunning all the missile-launching sites.

But by that time the secret war against Hitler was almost at an end. The great deceptions of Bodyguard had fulfilled their purpose. Allied Underground agents in France, Belgium, and Holland were coming out of hiding to rejoice in the liberation of their countries; the huge computer complex at Bletchley was chattering only rarely because, forced back into their own country, the Germans were using telephone lines rather than radio to communicate with and between units—which was why Ultra gave no warning of the last German offensive of the war, the Battle of the Bulge, in December 1944.

The war was almost at an end, but not quite. For the Germans still occupied large areas of Europe, including Denmark. And from Denmark in January 1945 came alarming news. The *Gestapo* had caught and arrested more than fifty of the leaders of the Princes, the Danish Underground organization. These men knew not only every detail of the Danish Resistance movement and the names and locations of many MI-6 agents in Copenhagen, some of them also knew the real significance of Dr. Bohr's research and where the atomic scientist had buried his vital papers in Carlsberg. It was too late now for Germany to manufacture an atomic bomb, but if the information fell into German hands it might well wind up in possession of the Russians, whose armies were advancing into the center of Hitler's "Thousand Year Reich." Despite the war-time agreement between the Allies and the Soviet Union to pool all technical information, the secret of the Manhattan Project had been purposely withheld from Stalin, for Churchill viewed the Soviet dictator's post-war ambitions in Europe with great suspicion, as did Roosevelt during the last months of his life.

The Danish Resistance chiefs were being held at *Gestapo* headquarters in central Copenhagen, a modern steel and concrete structure known as Shell House, once the Danish headquarters of the Shell Oil Company. There they would undergo daily torture until eventually and inevitably some of them talked. None of the Danes had suicide pills.

News of the disaster that had overtaken the Danish Underground was brought to London by Sven Truelsen, a Danish secret agent in MI-6 employ who had escaped to Sweden. He proposed that the RAF mount a precision attack against Shell House, skipping bombs into the base of the building so as to destroy the *Gestapo* files held there and also to permit the Danish prisoners, held on the building's top floor, to escape. When RAF commanders asked for a photograph of the target, Truelsen went back to Copenhagen, stole a boat, took the required photos from the sea (the attacking planes would be coming from that direction), and then once again made good his escape to Sweden.

With Truelsen's photos, postcards, maps, and other detailed information, a squadron of RAF Mosquito fighter-bombers practiced their hair-raising mission in England. Their attack would have to be precise, not only to be effective in destroying Shell House, but also to avoid hitting Danish civilian buildings, including a Catholic school nearby. Shortly before dawn on March 21, 1945, eighteen Mosquitoes, each carrying two delayed-action bombs, which would give the pilots eleven seconds to maneuver their aircraft away from the explosions, took off from England headed for Denmark.

The Mosquitoes swept in from the sea over Copenhagen just at dawn, swerving to avoid church steeples and power lines, a flight of American long-range Mustang fighters overhead giving protection. The first bombs blasted into the base of the Shell building precisely on target. Upstairs in their cells, the Danish Resistance chiefs watched the walls cave in upon them, but one of them retained presence of mind enough to get hold of the cell keys from a stunned German guard. In the ensuing uproar and confusion all the Danes escaped, though none at the time knew the fearful price paid for their freedom.

That price was exacted when one of the Mosquitoes crashed directly into the nearby Catholic convent school. The schoolyard was full of children and one of the nuns, Sister Gertrud, was pointing to the sky and shouting with excitement, "Look, children, the British!" Then the world exploded into blackness. One of the children, Merete Jensen, twelve years old at the time, would later recall, "We were all so jubilant because at last here were our friends flying in from the sea. Then there was a terrible crash and everything went dark and it seemed as if after that there was just a long silence. I thought maybe I am dead. So I sat waiting. And then I heard children crying and praying and crying and then suddenly there was the smell again of spring. It had been such a marvelous day, you know. The first day of spring . . ."

Twenty-seven teachers and eighty-seven children died on that first day of spring, the last victims of the secret war. Years later, when the RAF squadron commander made a visit to Copenhagen to try to explain to the parents of the dead children what had happened, the parents comforted him. They wanted him to know they felt the raid had been necessary.

EPILOGUE/THE LAST ILLUSION

Here, where sword United Nations drew,
Our countrymen were warring on that day!
And this is much—and all—which will not pass away.

BYRON,
CHILDE HAROLD'S PILGRIMAGE

The end of the secret war was not the end of secrecy. With Hitler dead in the ruins of Russian-occupied Berlin, with all of Germany prostrate at the feet of victorious Allied and Soviet armies, many of the secret agencies were disbanded, such as the Special Operations Executive (SOE), the Double-Cross Committee, Stephenson's BSC in New York, and, at a slightly later date, the American Office of Strategic Services (OSS). The great computers at Bletchley were silent and the cryptanalysts of the Golf, Cheese, and Chess Society returned to civilian, largely academic pursuits. Thousands of people had been party to the secret operations of Allied Intelligence, but, in the years of peace that followed, not one of them talked! The true story of the spy war against Nazi tyranny would remain unknown for thirty years, and even today parts of it are still shrouded in secrecy.

Buried behind the discretion of individuals and Britain's Official Secrets Act, the heroic story of the secret war was soon forgotten amid the dramas of a new conflict—the cold war between the United States and the Soviet Union. To confront this new threat the United States created an entirely new espionage and secret warfare organization, the Central Intelligence Agency (CIA), which for many years was headed by Allen Dulles, a veteran of World War II's OSS.

The world in which the CIA operated was in many ways far more complex than the world of 1939–1945. The enemies of freedom now were not mindless masses of what Churchill called "dull, drilled, brutish Hun infantry," led by intellectual thugs and madmen whose aims were genocidal. The values of democracy were threatened now by a system of thought and government that adopted most of the democratic vocabulary but gave such words as liberty, security, and democracy new and perverted meanings; a system that competed for the minds and allegiances of reasonable people, especially deprived and oppressed reasonable people. There was now no great moral crusade against an obviously satanic enemy such as Hitler; in place of that there was an endless competition, especially within the world's poorer nations, between communism and democracy in which the best weapons were not guns or plastic explosives but rather food, economic aid, and, above all, ideas.

Yet, too often the CIA, misinterpreting the lessons of World War II, has sought military solutions to political problems, has employed violence to combat ideals—a losing proposition, as the Nazis learned long ago. For no matter how detestable we may consider a system of thought, it can only be defeated by another system of thought, not by cyanide pellets, long-distance microphones, spy-in-the-sky satellites, or personal assassinations. Such weapons may be fit for use against the Soviet's ruthless intelligence agency, the KGB, but were the KGB to vanish tomorrow, the Communist system would still pose a grave threat to democratic values.

But the CIA, embroiled in the most complex of *political* struggles, has relied far more upon technique, weaponry, technology, and force than upon political analysis. An excellent example of where that can lead was the CIA-directed invasion of Cuba in 1960 that culminated in the Bay of Pigs disaster. Here the CIA employed a well-trained, well-equipped army of Cuban exiles in an attempt to topple the government of Fidel Castro. The assumption was that as soon as this army landed, the Cuban people would rise in revolt against Castro's regime. Everything went according to plan at first: Absolute secrecy was maintained; CIA agents inside Cuba (operating with equipment that would have dazzled MI-6's agents) fulfilled their tasks; the invasion force was landed on schedule and enjoyed, at first, the support of the U.S. Navy and disguised U.S. warplanes—yet it was doomed from the beginning. It was doomed because the CIA's political analysis of the situation was hollow. The Cuban people were not about to rebel against Fidel Castro at that time, especially in favor of an army of exiles and émigrés, many of them the very officials against whom they had risen under Castro's leadership just a few years earlier. The CIA relied upon technique and technology, not upon the minds and hearts of men, and was badly defeated.

And even when CIA operations were successful—as in reimposing the Shah of Iran's rule over his country after he had been expelled in 1952, or in toppling the democratically elected government of Salvadore Allende in Chile ten years later—these were disastrously expensive "triumphs" for which the American people have paid and will continue to pay in years to come.

The CIA is, of course, staffed by professionals, people whose primary ambition is to "get ahead" in their chosen field, not necessarily to pursue ideals. CIA leaders have often protested that they do not make policy; they simply provide policy "options" to their government and then faithfully execute whatever orders they are given. When those orders (such as the ones that caused the CIA to spy upon American citizens at home) arouse the wrath of Congress and the American people, CIA officials profess themselves puzzled and hurt, which only indicates a kind of political and moral illiteracy among them. Being masters of the means of secret warfare, they do not concern themselves with the ends to which it may be put. And this exaltation of means above ends is the last and basic illusion that today's spy masters have inherited from their misinterpretation of the secret war against Hitler.

For the long struggle against fascism waged by Allied Intelligence agencies was not a "game" of techniques played by indifferent professionals; it was the work of many thousands of dedicated amateurs, people whose talents and devotions were enlisted in a great cause: to secure the rights and freedoms of the individual against the colossus of the all-devouring state. They did not fight to ensure the primacy of an American copper company in Chile, the profits of an oil cartel in Iran, the security of sugar corporations in Cuba; they could never have been recruited for such ends.

Yet, the rights and freedom of the individual are in grave danger today, just as they were in 1939 and as they have always been throughout history. And it is as true today as it has ever been that the first line of defense for a democratic society is *information*. But the uses to which that information is put must serve democratic ends. Otherwise the struggle against tyranny loses its moral purpose and content.

This was the great lesson learned in the bloody classroom of the struggle against fascism that both the CIA and the postwar American governments it has served seem to have forgotten: that underground warfare cannot succeed outside the matrix of intelligent political direction and that in war, whether hot or cold, moral values are still supreme. For it was the morally informed commitment and dedication of individual citizens to worthy ideals of thousands of the free world that led them on dangerous, lonely, often fatal missions into the heart of Nazi darkness. Without their dedication to moral and spiritual values, that darkness might well have engulfed the world.

Alsop, Stewart, and Thomas Braden. *Sub Rosa*. New York: Harcourt, Brace & World, 1964.

Amort, C., and M. Jedlicka. *The Canaris File*. London: Wingate, 1970.

Aster, Sydney. *1939: The Making of the Second World War*. New York: Simon and Schuster, 1974.

Astley, Joan B. *The Inner Circle*. London: Hutchinson, 1971.

Attlee, Clement R. *As It Happened*. London: Heinemann, 1954.

Barkas, G. *The Camouflage Story*. London: Cassell, 1952.

Bartz, K. *The Downfall of the German Secret Service*. London: Kimber, 1956.

Bazna, Elyesa. *I Was Cicero*. New York: Harper & Row, 1962.

Bernstein, Jeremy. *The Analytical Engine*. New York: Random House, 1963.

Boveri, Margaret. *Treason in the 20th Century*. New York: Putnam, 1963.

Buckmaster, Maurice J. *Specially Employed*. London: Batchworth, 1952.

Bulloch, John. *M.I.5*. London: Barker, 1963.

Bullock, Alan. *Hitler—A Study in Tyranny*. New York: Harper & Row, 1963.

Carre, M.-L. *I Was the "Cat."* London: Four Square Books, 1961.

Cave Brown, Anthony. *Bodyguard of Lies*. New York: Harper & Row, 1975.

Collier, Richard. *Ten Thousand Eyes*. New York: Dutton, 1958.

Colvin, Ian. *Master Spy*. New York: McGraw-Hill, 1951.

Cookridge, E. H. *Inside S.O.E.* London: Barker, 1966.

Deacon, R. *A History of the British Secret Service*. London: Muller, 1969.

De Launay, J., ed. *European Resistance Movements, 1939–1945*. London: Pergamon, 1964.

Delmer, Sefton. *The Counterfeit Spy*. New York: Harper & Row, 1971.

Dulles, Allen W. *The Craft of Intelligence*. New York: Harper & Row, 1963.

Ehrlich, B. *The French Resistance*. London: Chapman & Hall, 1966.

Farago, Ladislas. *The Game of the Foxes*. New York: McKay, 1971.

Flicke, W.F. *War Secrets in the Ether*. Washington: NSA, 1954.

Foot, M.R.D. *S.O.E. in France*. London: HMSO, 1966.

Fuller, Jean Overton. *Madeleine*. London: Gollancz, 1952.

Garby-Czerniaski, Roman. *The Big Network*. London: Ronald, 1963.

Gehlen, Reinhard. *The Service*. New York: World, 1972.

Goerlitz, Walter. *History of the German General Staff*. New York: Praeger, 1953.

Hagen, Louis. *The Secret War for Europe*. New York: Stein and Day, 1969.

Haukelid, Knut. *Skis Against the Atom*. London: Kimber, 1954.

Howarth, P., ed. *Special Operations*. London: Routledge, 1955.

Hyde, H.M. *Cynthia*. London: Hamish Hamilton, 1966.

————. *Room 3603*. New York: Farrar, Straus, 1952.

Ingersoll, R. *Top Secret*. New York: Harcourt Brace, 1946.

Irving, David. *The German Atomic Bomb*. New York: Simon and Schuster, 1968.

James, Clifton. *I Was Monty's Double*. London: Rider, 1954.

Kahn, David. *The Codebreakers*. New York: Macmillan, 1967.

Kirkpatrick, Lyman B. *The Real CIA*. New York: Macmillan, 1968.

Lewin, Ronald. *Rommel as Military Commander*. London: Batsford, 1969.

————. *Ultra Goes to War*. New York: McGraw-Hill, 1978.

Manvell, Roger. *Conspirators*. New York: Ballantine, 1971.

Masterman, J.C. *The Double-Cross System in the War of 1939–1945*. New Haven: Yale University Press, 1972.

Montagu, Ewen. *The Man Who Never Was*. London: Evans, 1966.

Morgan, Sir F. *Overture to Overlord*. London: Hodder & Stoughton, 1950.

Pash, Boris. *The Alsos Mission*. New York: Award, 1969.

Pinto, Orestes. *Friend or Foe?* New York: Putnam, 1954.

Popov, Dusko. *Spy-Counterspy*. New York: Grosset & Dunlap, 1974.

Robertson, Terrence. *Dieppe: The Shame and the Glory*. London: Hutchinson, 1963.

Rowan, Richard & Robert Deindorfer. *The Secret Service*. New York: Hawthorne, 1967.

Schlabrendorff, Fabian von. *The Secret War Against Hitler*. London: Hodder & Stoughton, 1966.

Stanford, Alfred B. *Force Mulberry*. New York: Morrow, 1951.

Stevenson, William. *A Man Called Intrepid*. New York: Harcourt Brace Jovanovich, 1976.

Strong, Sir Kenneth. *Intelligence at the Top*. New York: Doubleday, 1969.

Sweet-Escott B. *Baker Street Irregular*. London: Methuen, 1965.

Tickell, J. *Moon Squadron*. London: Wingate, 1956.

Turing, S. *Alan M. Turing*. Cambridge: Heffer, 1959.

Wiener, Jan G. *The Assassination of Heydrich*. New York: Pyramid, 1969.

Wingate, Sir Ronald. *Not in the Limelight*. London: Hutchinson, 1959.

Winterbotham, Frederick W. *Secret and Personal*. London: Kimber, 1969.

————. *The Ultra Secret*. New York: Harper & Row, 1974.

Woolcombe, R. *The Campaigns of Wavell, 1939–1943*. London: Cassell, 1959.

Young, Desmond. *Rommel, the Desert Fox*. New York: Harper & Bros., 1950.

The best overall history of the struggle against Hitler remains Winston Churchill's magisterial *The Second World War,* in six volumes, available in paperback from Bantam Books, New York. It is instructive to see what Churchill, writing just after the war, does *not* tell by comparing his work with the equally magisterial history of secret operations during the conflict, Anthony Cave Brown's *Bodyguard of Lies,* in two volumes, published by Harper & Row, New York, in 1975, *after* the expiration of the British Official Secrets Act. A side of secret operations not covered in the Cave Brown book is brilliantly set forth by William Stevenson in *A Man Called Intrepid,* available in paperback from Ballantine Books, New York. For the story of the Turing engine, consult Winterbotham's *The Ultra Secret* and Lewin's *Ultra Goes to War.* For those who wish to delve more deeply into some of the stories told herein, there are such books as Fuller's *Madeleine* and Hyde's *Cynthia,* all of which are listed in the bibliography.

INDEX

Robert Goldston is the author of many highly acclaimed titles, most recently *The Sword of the Prophet* and *The Road Between the Wars: 1918–1941*, both published by Dial. His other books include *The Russian Revolution, The Life and Death of Nazi Germany,* and *The Rise of Red China,* all of which were ALA Notable Books.

Mr. Goldston was born in New York City and attended Columbia University. A former Guggenheim Fellow, he has written novels and documentary films in addition to his historical works.

Mr. Goldston has traveled extensively and lived in England, France, and Spain. He now lives with his family in Upstate New York.